breccia

BRECCIA
selected poems 1972-1986

Pierre Joris

© Pierre Joris 1975, 1976, 1977, 1978, 1979, 1980, 1982, 1983, 1986, 1987 and 2014

Published in Great Britain in 2014 by Skylight Press,
210 Brooklyn Road, Cheltenham, Glos GL51 8EA

First published in 1987 in Luxembourg by Editions PHI and in the USA by Station Hill Press.

All rights reserved. Except for the quotation of short passages for the purposes of criticism and review, no part of this publication may be reproduced, stored in a retrieval system or transmitted, in any form or by any means, electronic, mechanical, photocopying, recording or otherwise, without the prior consent of the copyright holder and publisher.

Pierre Joris has asserted his right to be identified as the author of this work.

Designed and typeset by Rebsie Fairholm
Publisher: Daniel Staniforth
Cover painting by Allen Fisher

www.skylightpress.co.uk

Printed and bound in Great Britain by Lightning Source, Milton Keynes

British Library Cataloguing-in-Publication data: a catalogue record for this book is available from the British Library.

ISBN 978-1-908011-88-6

CONTENTS

Eric Mottram: OASIS AND CROSSROADS	7
PREFACE TO BRECCIA	13
from ANTLERS	15
A BUNDLE OF RODS BOUND UP WITH AN AXE IN THE MIDDLE, ITS BLADE PROJECTING	37
SCREENS	38
from HEARTHWORK	42
10 A.M.	72
EVENING	74
ANGUISH, A RIDDLE	75
LOVE SONG	75
OUT OF THE DEEP…	75
UNTITLED	76
THE ANGLE & THE DIRECTIONS	76
MIDNIGHT IN CAMBRIDGE	77
SUNDAY MORNING POEM	77
SORE THUMB	78
from TRACING	79
BRECCIA	100
MAHLER'S QUINCUNX	103
THE BOOK OF LUAP NALEC	107
MATROSEN LIED	127
TANITH FLIES	131

WRITING / READING 1. *via Bruno*	145
WRITING / READING 2. *via Michel Foucault*	147
WRITING / READING 3. *via Jacques Derrida*	150
WRITING / READING 4. *via Canguilhem*	152
WRITING / READING 5. *via Robert Kelly*	155
WRITING / READING 6. *via Robert Duncan*	157
BODY COUNT	164
THE BROKEN GLASS	167
from MAKE IT UP LIKE SAY	175
MEANING A MONKEY	175
PUT YOUR FACE ON	180
YEARS AGO, TUNISIA	182
THE TIME FACTOR IN SCIENCE FICTION MOVIES	184
CARTE DU TENDRE	185
ORE BEFORE IT IS DRESSED	187
WINDOW PUN	189
ENGLISH LANDSCAPE	194
TADPOLE STRATEGIST	195
DHÛ'L-RUMA	196
GERMAN LANDSCAPE, REVISITED	197
FIN-DE-SIÈCLE IDENTIKIT	198
THE HORSES OF LALLA FATIMA	203
1. MEDITATION IN A KITCHEN	203
2. THE TALE	207
Postface	212

Eric Mottram: OASIS AND CROSSROADS
— *An Introduction for Pierre Joris*

For the cover of his *Tracing* – 1975 poems published in 1982 – Pierre Joris provided a set of rapid gists as a map of his life since 1946, including:

> •18 years Luxembourg: 2 Paris: 4 New York: 3 Constantine: 8 London: tomorrow elsewhere: distrust vertical roots, history: the spread is horizon(t)al rhizomes: root gives / is stalk stem branch flower: no direction favoured a priori…. think that resistance essential mode of action today.

Europe, North Africa, America – and as the opening poem of *Tracing* says, "(there is no such / thing as West)". The diagram of root into flower may well be a misleading set of separations rather than transformations of a life. Joris has necessarily to consider carefully his whereabouts. His poetry does precisely this. His languages – and his translations of Celan, Kerouac, Corso and many others are exemplary – are both negotiable, communicative and problematic, since his poetry is in English. And in an English which has no dialect, and remains poised between American and British. But then his inheritance of poetics is mainly from "projective verse" (after Charles Olson's seminal summary of the 1950 position after Pound and Williams) and "open field" (again, largely an American legacy from the mid-twentieth century's poetics). But of course these poetics themselves draw on some European forces. Joris turned his knowledge of such techniques into his own vehicles of enquiry and song. His mobility is converted into a highly reflective, often inturned poetry, essentially analytic of what his sensibility is doing *now*, in *this* place from which he senses he will soon remove, with *this* new information to be made personally active. "Resistance essential mode of action," but with a major proviso in a poem of 1981: "a situation where we use force as a means of communication / a crisis teaches us nothing."

Joris's poetry is part of his life-work as communicator. His translations of American literature have entered the French sphere. He co-edited and translated a pioneering text of contemporary British poets, *Voix-Off/Angleterre*, in 1980, and then added, in 1984, to these services with a fine anthology, co-edited with Paul Buck, *Matières d'Angleterre*, a bilingual collection of texts which remains the best introduction to British poetry that resists the culture's deadly conformism. In 1974 he edited, with W.R Prescott, an issue of their magazine *Sixpack* dedicated to the American poet and centre of New York poetic culture Paul Blackburn – it remains an essential introduction. Joris knows what has to be done, and this is one of his ways of ascertaining where he is. His confrontation with the Tassili inscriptions has to be a participation respecting ancient artists in another culture as examples of his own condition. From Constantine, Algeria, he writes in a letter of 1976 with a characteristic sense of needing to understand something of another people beyond mere tourism – and through this to move his own work into another stage of vision and method:

The Words of Yourougou deals with Dogon cosmology ... It consists of 2 parallel series of 24 poems each, where every Dogon "word" is associated with specific plants, animals, myths & techniques (such as tilling, weaving, grinding etc.). The attempt is to *break* the constricting magic number sequence which weaves the Dogon world view into a more than coherent whole, by using the number correspondences to build a musical scheme that lets invention in.

At the same time he is working on part two of the *Antlers* sequence, teaching at the University of Constantine, reading texts on language, Dumézil's *Mythe et Épopée*, Eckerman's *Gespräche mit Goethe*, re-working the Paul Celan translations, reading Shelley, making a journey into the oases of Souf, and much more.

So that Joris's poetry emerges within an active, varied cultural life – specific poems as moments of penetrative self-estimation as critical estimation of the problems of the culture within which he is mobile, unrooted rather than uprooted, and yet consistently involved. In this sense, he is very much a late twentieth-century poet, outside the limits of nationalism, the parameters of limitation which wreck official poetry scenes, the legitimacies of prizes and government grants.

But English is his creating instrument – as he puts it in *Antlers*, "… after all these changes. / I'm still an / espontaneo, / though I've made it my profession. / & who is to say / it could have been different?" In this book, some of the stag myths of Europe serve as a narrative armature, but they revert to a boyhood hunt experience, an early intuition – now recognized forcibly – of the desire for an adventurous, willed manhood. The hunt now includes a kind of suffering in the grown man which is necessarily complex and ambivalent. The myths are within consciousness, subjected to resistance, and the whole action rendered into the analytic projections of poetry. Knowledge includes resistances – "The community knows & exiles the / Saturnian."

In the Algerian bases of *Tanith Flies* (1978), Joris recalls "obsessions … my deer & foxes" as "a way to see through / the opaqueness of our selves / a way to look at / the transparency of the world." He senses now "the languages / pull timeward." This time the local myth to be regarded is Tanis, great goddess of North Africa and Phoenicia, and her signs. Like Artemis in *Antlers*, she ambivalently confers energies and threatens well-being. But in addition: "three separated spectres settled like horns on our heads" – and then a Joris motif re-emerges in its full ambiguity, syntactical and sexual: "and watching we sipped our coffees / caught in the net woven by / the dead talk of the unlaid." The flies live on remains, and are both scavengers and "fear-flies," death reminders, echoing back to the Greek Furies on the other side of the Middle Sea:

> life is spontaneous
> creation in that sense
> spontaneous putrefaction
> out of which
> we rise into our day

This kind of layered impersonal statement achieves its finest management in *Tracing* – but still explorative and unstable enough to produce a lively volume of entrances and exits. In Henri Michaux's terms from *Passage*, "I write in order to traverse myself." Rites of passage are traced, and in his characteristic way, the poet plays on the layers in his title word. In the first poem, "Tyre" attracts the Joris reader into his Mediterranean scene from earlier work — and "the Maya" introduces a reiterated theme: "mobility of every / man & woman." The "place" of the book is now to one side of the world's decay and conflict systems, so interlocking and manic. "No stars fixed… No gods fixed" is precisely the opposite of the crazed world of 1982. The confident poetics of *Tracing* is itself resistant to being sacrificed to Thanatos. Mobility is a form of survival: "the dream of the new / language, needed / if we are to go on … arises not from an already formed / speech, but out / of the necessity / of speech." Place is to be created by this man on the road: "place we have retraced /our steps to / so that now /I may arise / from you / my crucible."

Joris is not a man to model himself on any particular. The cover of *Le Livre de Luap Nalec* (1986) states his position well enough: "Paul Celan en spectre de l'autre côté du miroir que lui tend son double, Pierre Joris. Un Joris passeur de langues, européen décalé, passé aux riches heures de la nuit américaine." But the poems tell a closer truth: "Face / myself/ past the bright / wound mirror?" – and: "I, / the Shifter, am spoken / through / these chambers—." Celan's poetics break convention, invent, go through the existent language systems, and therefore through the social systems – and that is what Joris knows he needs to do, in both translations and transmissions. This is his liaison with Celan. And *Trans* – that favourite suffix of Mark Rothko – is the key term. Celan/Nalec is the site where Joris's uses of language meet in a viable transition between antecedent and future. And in mid-text, there is placed a typical set of verbal definitions in several languages, and drawing on key bases for three key generic terms. The goal is "a different song."

Joris's most recent book, *Goodbye To England* (1987) opens afloat and still enquiring – on a ship at sea, "taking stock" – and continues into the area of *Trans*: "outside" and "inside" interpenetrative. The mobile man speaks once again: "the / seanoise with / me always." His "New Poems" in this most welcome "Selected Poems" continue to develop his floating world – and particularly his concisely measured lineal forms – notably in "Window Pun." And he continues to draw from his sense of the stable flexibility of the English language he revels in – "a sentenced / sentense" ("Body Count," 1979), "The E / on any stone / is revealed by a kiss / reveiled / by a priest, / reviled / if displaced" (*Tracing*) – the very words have to be held inside the enquiry they represent, within intellectual curiosity and sensuousness. A mobile density of language gives an urgency to Joris's discourse at its best, a need to hold protean experience long enough to identify at least partially. The penultimate poem in the selection, "Fin-de-siècle Identikit," includes his usual ambivalence towards England – the place in which he has moved his poetry most significantly, made good friends, had his own house, and yet found the culture too self-contained, too uncritical, and – it is an accusation in the poem – too idyllic in its seductive green places. Various countries make ghost appearances, and then back comes the poet to language, his life-line, the instrument of transformation, of resistances to "a single-minded community." An Englishman might well suggest some modifications here, but there is no question of the force of the poem. In the final work, "The Horses of Lalla Fatima," the settling programme is the road: "risked ... yesterday ... tomorrow," a "rest in the oasis;" a cooked etymology which constructs needed words; antlers become forks, and the ideal place is "choice at the crossroads."

The poem in fact concerns the impossibility of single-directional fiction of any kind, and the need to resist single interpretation. Pierre Joris's book cannot be ended.

PREFACE TO BRECCIA

This collection gathers work written over a fourteen year period & aims at making a book, that is, a coherence. Much has been left out, though *Breccia* does contain the major part of what I would wish to save from that period. Some of the sequences, like *Antlers* or *Tracing*, have by now run their course & are represented here by selections that I hope will show their specific thrusts while reticulating the book at hand. Others, like *Luap Nalec* or *Tanith Flies*, are offered complete. Others still, like *Writing/Reading* are open-ended series & point beyond the closure a retrospective collection such as this inevitably suggests. A few sequences or 'books' (such as *A Book of Common Places* and *An American Suite*) from the early to late seventies have been left out for lack of space, while the mass of short poems written over that period has had to be whittled down for the same reason.

 What I would have liked to see come through in *Breccia* is the tension between the fragmentary nature of experience & knowledge, & the desire for a narrative syntax, for the whole story of the tribe, the telling of which does inevitably blur the sharp edges of those shards. Europe gave me my history, those ghostly voices of the ancestors, real or made up, lied to or listened to. America gave me geography, the space of my dance. My hope has been that language, or what little of it I have been able to serve, has made a threshing floor for their marriage.

 This book is the first I publish in Luxembourg, the country I am from, & at the same time the first I publish in America, the continent I am returning to after the apprentice years & books in England. The occasion feels accurate in its pointing to this condition of between I & the work seem to inhabit & share.

Paris, France
August 1987.

BRECCIA: 1: a rock consisting of sharp fragments embedded in a fine-grained matrix (as sand or clay)
2: an agglomerate deposit of debris in a cave or other site occupied by prehistoric man .

OUR LAST CHANCE IS THIS: HIDE NOTHING
George Oppen

The net is not the world; it is the imagination of the world.
Robert Duncan

Nous n'existons, ne parlons et ne travaillons, de raison, de science et de bras, que dans et par l'écart à l'équilibre. Tout est écart à l'équilibre, hormis le rien. C'est-à-dire l'identité.
Michel Serres

from ANTLERS

for Eric Mottram

I.

Just one more -
        one more
  maybe before
this night
takes over -
       the necessary strength:
  words, things
that are words
coming
or is it
that I don't know
  if they are
coming or going
        anymore.
But there is
something here
antlers
        maybe
the word is antlers:
     a piercing
from behind.
Or am I playing
courting
  danger & anger
- doing battle
      with wills pitched -
patching the hole
the antlers tore?

The antler is not
my will
            it is what
drives me.

In Norway
I bought reindeer
antlers from a
drunken Lapp.
   That was more
than long
ago.
           They are still
& not mounted,
mildewed
next to the cracked flower
pots in the room
we called the
'dry-room'
            though it was
the wettest place
in the house.

This is the story
the first word
gave back
after all
these changes.
I'm still an
espontaneo
   though I've
made it
my profession.
           & who is to say
it could have been
different?

      It is not
that I'm satisfied
or
dissatisfied
    I am
myself
      & take it
that any way
I may define
myself
     is the truth
of that moment.
Not
      that it matters.
It does
  but that in turn
  does not.

       We move
to another
  light
      (not the bright/
  white cross
between the mildewed
        eyes)

  a different dance
    by & with
      a volition
changed by time
but the brightness the
claritas
       remains
unchanged .
        It only changes
when we
stand still.

      When we don't follow
the sun
          behind the mountains
        the sun
sinks into the ocean
         behind the mountains.

II.

      Until his hounds may tare that heart of his in twain
      Which thus torments us harmless Harts
      And puts our hearts to pain.
        George Turberville, 1575

    Though it
may take time
       to learn how to
run
without
          getting
! the antlers
        caught
in the undertow
or how not to
be cornered
by the hounds
of cold Artemis -
      that time too
part of the necessary
  distance
       we have to deal with
between here & dying.

        Artemis knows
how to tell
the age of a stag

from the height
at which the tree's bark
had been broken
open by the antlers.
    St. Hubertus
never was able
 to take sides -
or was it
that he just didn't
  have the power
to break her arrows?
His magic
the bright
   /
    white
  cross
between eyes & antlers
Ha!
   an easy
target
   under the full moon.

Startled the stag
moves on
    buries
his antlers
in the night.
The fool moon! on
  a drunken Lap's face.

Further South
  (Tongres
  (Maastricht
  (Liège
   the evangelical
hunting grounds
  of Hubertus.

On November 3rd
  each
      November
in his honour
we kill
deer
& make of their antlers
knifehandles
hatstands
bone meal.

    There came a time
when the women
didn't want
the heads
on the wall
anymore:
    it scares
the kids,
the glass eyes &
that bright
      /
        white
    cross
shines at midnight
under the full moon.
    The antlered heads
catch dust
in the attic.
    Spiderwebs span
the distance
    from point
to point.

    St. Hubert
drunk
    chases Artemis

along the makeshift
table
     at the forest's edge.
The deer hang
from the trees
     high enough
to keep the dogs
at bay.
   The hunters live
on pork
        venison
on Sunday only
once a month.
     The young man's
initiation:
     to break
open
the slain deer.
My bone-handle knife.

   'Look, son,
it's all
a matter of
accuracy:
     the sharp edge
on
     the thin line
& if you hit it right
you crack
the bone
with one blow.'
     The hind legs
fall sideways
open & steaming.
Artemis shudders
her eyes
on the dogs.

        You
push your hands
into the opening
carefully
slit the belly
remove the guts
watch the dogs
they may lick
the blood
but don't let them
tear the entrails
or you'll get shit
all over.

       I learned all this
early
       I was eager
wanting antlers.

If you walk
through the woods
at a specific time
of the year
       you'll find
any amount
of discarded antlers.

       Artemis shuns
them, her arrow-
heads are made
of steel &
her hounds eat
pork.
       St. Hubert, St. Hubert
you goddam fool
running through the woods
you've got horns

all over your
head
       & your back
is spiked
with arrows.

V.

> *First image of Saturn. A man with a stag's
> head, on a dragon with an owl which is eating
> a snake in his right hand.*
> Giordano Bruno   De Umbris Idearum

The horned man
      first dream of
darkness
below the stars
above the earth.

There is no way
we can avoid
dealing
with that aspect.
      I mean Ficino
was a good man
but afraid
        whereas
Bruno
knew better or
more or
was not afraid.

      The antlers! Shadows
in the memory

a dark mossy
tree comes
      out of /
from /
      the night.
Moss crawling
with transparent
creatures
      (the white
creatures, cross
of the night.

      The hunter
counts
the points
to know the age
of the stag.
      The pearls
around the antlers'
base
      a measure of
strength
&
power.
The moral
wealth said
to lie
in the branches
the quantity
number
thereof.
      When antlers
are branchless
the stag's a
freak
creature,
      called killer-

stag
the white killer
of the woods
    (the branches
keep life in
the autumn play -
they can't
dig in deep
enough
    can't reach
the quick.
    The white, straight
dagger-
antlers tear
the guts).
    The stag
-afflicted thus -
knows & roams
alone
    comes out
late on the fall
meadow
    comes out
a cold knowledge
& a blazing white
something
between
the eyes : the frozen
pain
    the freak
creature knows
has known
  all his life
    from the inside
out
has known
  all his death

is in the shadow
the outside
            casts
(a heavy-handed
spell)
            on that other
knowledge
        old as bone
& his by chance
of growth
of bone.

            He comes out late
moves in silence
through the shadows
of the tree-line
wants to
stay
        there to
live his separated
path
        winding
along that
weaving across
        that inter
face
        that skin
- a cool & porous
place -
            links the
private forest
to the public
land.
        But the shadows
betray the secret
creature:
            against

their dark
surface
  the blazing
white something
stands
   out clear,
reveals the stag's
presence
to the watchful
herd.
  Proud
& many-pronged
the leader
   turns
away from his
does
  moves against
that light
   has to
challenge
what he does not
know,
   has to
overcome his fears
to keep an
old ritual
alive.

   After
the kill
the stag
moves on moves
in
  deeper into
the woods
   away
from the does

circling the dead
16-pointer
      away
from the unleashed
hounds
        the hunter
sets on his trail
feeling cheated
of his prize
      - the kill
he has waited for
has counted on
          too
long -.

Cornered
      in the heart
of the forest
        the stag
fights the dogs
who know the danger
but don't mind
or care
        blinded
to the tearing
pain.   Their frenzy
pales only
      in the agony
of their bodies
impaled
      on the
perfectly
pearled
daggers
      of bone &
silence.

   Breathless &
bruised, falling
over roots the inner
forest's darkness
hides
   the hunter
closes in.
     He drags
the wounded
dogs back
   & crazed
by the loss
of his priceless
pack
   he lays
a ring of
fire
   around
the stag

who dies

    in the heart
of a blaze.

VI.

    But the image, the
actual
image remains:
   the heat
does not
consume the
antlers .

       The fire
covers
the antlers
             &
      the fire
occults
the bright
        /
          white
something
sign
(of)
the creature
's wider dream,
      the too-
bright diamond
that is
returned to
black
      to the true
colour of
carbon.

      It is not
as trophies
for the killer
that the antlers
remain.
      The owls
will see
to that, the guardians
of the heart
      of the forest
watch
      from the trees
lining the
charred

clearing,
> dark new eye

at the centre
of,
> opening at

the centre of
his death.

> The antlers
> remain.

A signature clearer
than diamond.
> Moon-branches

& growths
between the daggers.

> The community knows

& exiles the
Saturnian.
> Bruno, nearby

at Oxford, defeats
the rich & healthy
scholastic minds.
> Antlers that

don't mesh
> different designs

& more.

X.

to James Fenimore Cooper

  in (& out of
bed
 /
  lam of child-
hood :
   hoodlum years
an encore for Uncas
  I was
Uncas son of the Great Snake
 as we all are
  sons of the Great Snake.

Uncas I was all ear
  who heard the cry
 of the caribou
a song
 200 years x
  4000 miles
removed
  /
   moved through under
tow & brush
toward
 the caribou
 : the perfectly bio
-de & up-
gradable
   matter to make
  anything
    needed.

like : antlers
  give

                knife
                  &
                scraper
wch in turn
   make possible
          total use
of anything else
i.e. everything
           ("verschlungen mit
                   Haut & Haaren")
                        the caribou is/has
                     to offer
& does.

Stalking a vision:
   the startled field
           mouse grows
out of
   all proportions
              the grown-ups
assume
   to be the measure
which is not any kind
of measure
or at best nothing
but the measure
of their own mediocrity
           for the measure
that is true
   is the measure
that moves / carries
        me / my, all my
eyes from here
   to further.

Uncas knew
          & for the perversion

  of the grey man
    for the purpose
  of the art form
    had to be/
to die/
   be killed
  die young be made
that figure
    , mounted , made
safe, the only
  measure
the grownups know
how to play
  how to take
know as the pale / fake
     image of continuity.

(where rhythm
means death
there is no
such thing
as rhythm)

       the periodic
      prongs of
     the antlers
    are not death
       are not identical
        replicas rhythmically
         wiping each
          other out
are not matter
 & anti-matter meeting
  at the barn-dance
   of chaos
: are growth / the measure of

year after year
the changes noted in the shapes
of the years
are the shapes
of the antlers
made new
    yet carriers
    of the whole

    the genes of
    total bone . But

the Delaware's hut
burned, the Delawares
wiped out,
the turtle sunk,
the Serpent drunk

    & the tail swallows the head
     for a change.

XI.

for William Prescott
(Oct. 4th 1973
Calais–Paris train

a map

or more:

        a topography

        where all the roads

end

in midair

complete

A BUNDLE OF RODS BOUND UP WITH AN AXE IN THE MIDDLE, ITS BLADE PROJECTING

(to & against NOB

killed an owl with a crooked arrow
pierced an owl seven separate places
made the faceless sky a person
to do this he who tries must be king
or fail for leatherbag is not windbag
but chaos killed sevenfold for
possibilities of rebirth &
pure ritual creation in the making
of all as is condensed in the glyph
before the diluting fall into metaphor
a fall put the poet the maker into
the hands of the king a bundle of
letters the law of the assembled
like acorns assemble the sows or
not like but still the glyph distilled
in place of which is nowhere & only
in time & first letter is a matter
a pure matter & simple thing though not
simpler than simple that is complex
enough to create attraction from which
is created the city which is syntax
& as we fumbling through the actual
fall into a metaphor became the bungled
bundle the fasces bound with wet
leatherstraps torn from the poisonous
windbag's soft underbelly dried in
king's hot speech contract they shrink
breaking the arrows' crookedness
forcing the straight narrow
the fake simple the slack syntax

SCREENS

1.
'L'embarras du choix' a lie
choice does not embarrass is
not encumbrance but is the
essential precondition of fullness
the possibility that makes
possibilities possible the posse
from latin *posse* to be able to
he is able to do it where it
is not one or single but
many any one or number he
chooses Composition
is the order of choice the chosen
possibles set out clear on the
screen numerous all he can
do & will do to compose
is to play as in play it by
ear but being numerous he
wants to has to play it by
ear nose eye play it by the whole
body to compose toward fullness
a curve of all that enters as
against the old posse rode a straight
line from nowhere to
nowhere & never did
get there the infinite horizontal
figure eight the horizontal stretch
of their cowboy hats capped by
the five gallon crown greasy
windbag the whole hat held tight
fixed to their heads a strap cutting
into the skin of their cheeks wedged

firm fixed forever under the square
jaws a barbed wire sweat band
all holds barred eight riders circling
a straight line forever strapped
to their Universal Studio hobbyhorses the
cameras move on rails move by
the riders shoot them shoot their fake motion
move out of sight at the end of the reel

2.
composition will clarify the issues
make light of the riders' possibilities
in the cutting room the dim lights he can
hardly see the numbers he chose
to order the composition he sings to himself
& finds the eight upside down cannot
make sense walks into bright
daylight screen of streetscene a real
policeman in a five gallon hat shoots
a random passerby he says he did not see
the man pointing out the drooping rim
of the hat speaks of marred visibility
pushes the hat back with the gun's barrel
a gesture he was taught at the movies still
he cannot see postures proudly his belief
that he never has & never will loose
his composition & understands it all but
a man of action has no patience for words
a gun speaks truer he says & aren't
the words in the paper also cast of
lead turning to the victim he says I
had no choice it was the law of chance
was against you blame it on yourself it was
your own choice to pass by here when you could

have stayed home the tableau freezes
a still life with a real stiff at the end of
the second reel the subreal not shot
that sequence as the cameras' rails do not
curve into this do not face into
this dimension of the total composition
unaware of which a deaf sound man cracks a can
of laughter a canister of laughing
gas tears the screen the keystone cops
applaud the killer a faded dissolve
another salvo the composition opens up
takes in the filmmaker who does not know
he too is included as is the rest of
the picture as his picture is included &
play back on the split screen
of the greatest possibilities outlined a
curve the infinite curve where silver
turns to gold via lead & gold
into solid air mirroring the
Universal picture moving picture of
all the transformations the human eye
is capable of where seeing is doing when
the distance of object to viewer is understood
or seen as the optical illusion it is the
concrete proposition being made is the offer
to junk all zoom lenses adjuncts &c props
of the dispelled illusion thereby to further

3.
vision as against prophecy the zoom into the painted backdrop
called future vision a close-up of now a total view
exploding viewfinder & lightmeter the cameramen released
dance a vision made new a forgotten posse gallops against
a moving carpet of straight lines shifted into neutral the lid

of a soundproof can locks the players into a 3-d postcard
picture of an abolished past the can flattened by the hoofs
of their horses transparent picture on the screen for a moment
flickers & fades they will never catch the villain
the hero will never arrive in time or on mainstreet to save
the maiden caught in the still life of a pastoral rape scene
the whip forever suspended in mid-air forever left hanging
above the wetback's back the blind producer's real cigar
touches the edge of the film goes up in flames the posse
is burned in the absence of a way out of the straight line the hero
is burned in the absence of a way out of the bad script the cop
is burned in the absence of a way out of his handcuffs the producer
is burned in the absence of a way out of his inability to see
this fire as part of the composition of the larger process
the total picture moving picture of necessary transformations
an alchemy of vision is act of & on vision act here not as in
actors' studio not as in last act first scene not as in to act in
a movie tho all these dimensions be included as specific
instances chromatic variations necessary for the total picture
whose totality is not acted or played or projected but is
its own projection as well as its own screen a screen
transparent to itself because inside of part of the picture
where an act is a hand-held eye we know there are eyes at the end
of our fingers where cinema becomes or is vérité
composition the endless exhilaration of all
the possible transformations an infinite series of stills
that are never only still but joined in the joyful dance
linked by the only true passion which is true movement
unencumbered by brakes & clutches cogs & rails here
composition has become vision where the only limit is
the injunction that the only thing that is impossible
that cannot enter the dance is a possibility that has not been used

1/1/1974

from HEARTHWORK

for Robert Kelly

    place of
seed & syllables :
            they are
what it is
all about.
        swarming / all about
the multitude of morning
embers   fire-particles
    the swarm, the warm
  animals dancing
    circling
the flames.

       warm-blooded, thus this round
& dance,
    how to, how to stomp,
  how to work
fire from earth.

      futharks & fire
    incunabula *nel mezzo*
mi retrovai

```
                    the way is the voice
        not 'sotto'
                        middle
                            ear the in . ter . mediate
place,
        mezzanine,
                    still centre
                            heaped earth matters
                                where the hair is parted
                            now ends sing,
                                    singed for mis-
                managing the fire
                we pass
                thru :
                again & a
gain.
            (thos, 'listening with the heart'


            hearth work is heap, heat / the slag
of the daily life,
                    the cinders needed
                    cradle of tomorrow's fire
            the small eternal matter
                the measure
                    flares up!
That sings at night, & sinks
into the night where
mornings you cannot find
the fire.
Waking up to its absence.
Because you cannot see
because you cannot feel
the fire you think
the fire
        is dead.
```

Late riser in an age where
your first light is cold
grey ooze through glass
a substance resents the heat
of fire in the absence of
sand, or earth.

The fire does not resent you
the fire has run to its earth
bright red fox
watched you sleep
through the night
eyes half closed
half open
at the first sign of dawn
turns white
hides in its earth.

Lids of grey cinder
say you were wrong
and will know it soon enough -
the fire is red underneath the earth
the fire is waiting
at the centre.

Spoke of the wheel
that has come full turn
you rise & look
for the centre.

   You find it
it is hard earth, the pounded circle
of crafted earth or stone
brick crucible
    où couve le feu

here fire hatches earth
under cover of

        *

    the way you come in
is the way you
leave:
        you carry your door
    (that's what it's for
   or the how
      of the word)
across the ditch, the heaped up
earth,
    mundus,
        the world.

        *

     aORTa

a place away runs
to the heart,
      comes (bi-valved
   to the hearth

the artful stone

     (a heart of stone
     is a hard fact

     a hot act

     a fire work
at work in
the crucible

       the crux   (or heart
of the matter

         the inspiration, the
         air pumped thru, then
the necessary breath-
ing out,
      breezing down the sadder
the blue
roads,
    the veins
  another way away

"*t'as de la veine*"
       (you are lucky

if by chance
you know
the whole
route.
      "The light lasts on out of history or memory
      in the face & turn of head toward the sink
      that endlessness of every day
      that is precisely eternity"

*

REAL   LAND

a/head
underfoot

*

the dream of two nights ago keeps coming back: sitting beside a large open fireplace, I am leafing through a big bulky album. Each photo is a snapshot of Jonathan Williams, naked. All are taken in indoor and outdoor locations that are completely unknown to me. On every photo Jonathan assumes a different pose & a different age. What puzzled me most was that in each shot he was accompanied by a bird — I remember a variety of species: a sparrow, a pigeon, a finch, a gull, a robin — perching each time on a different part of Jonathan's anatomy.

*

Sun is matter
a pure matter of
getting there, that
is (to) morning
the rise or erection
of the sun-matter
two are all
that's needed
to take aim
two measure
distance, set
the relation-
ship
  straight
on its curved
course,
   let the sun
take its course,
    first second
second & third
cause
  & at four
in the afternoon

        the foregoing begins
        to dim,
                the actual
setting
sets in -
we are on set
with our curved snouts
our square ears our
pleistocene eyes
we are
the race can stare
the sun in the eye
(wch is not staring
at the sun)
we are brothers
to the creatures
that live in the sun
who is the matter
or mater, the
mother of us all.

        *

The new spine of Europa located : the
Urals, the Ural-Caucasus complex where
Kundalini sleeps coiled in the Black Sea.
Any mappemonde for the reinvention of
Europe has to start there. That
hotbed hot enough, no need to go
further South (i.e. the so-called
cradle of Civ., Meso-potamia, is but a
parallel development in time (tho
its space leads to a different use, uses
of, a different sense of, communitas,
of, 'city'.

        *

        &, further back of us, futharks,
            multiple, not single
     origins of us, our 'humanitas' : the
invention of fire
        equals / is coterminous w/
           the discovery of city

     to work fire from earth
        the mundus, ditch, & the earth thrown up
          ring of earth around the fire

              the hearth
                is the city

        *

*"It is the event of a momentary sequence
that depended upon the place it had in common
    among common places, the daily routine
of suffering, pleasure, respite & makeshift companions."*

        *

drink the red wine
in the white house

tracing the contour
of this brew, this

bruised summer after
noon, pending —

        *

*"the leaves can be trusted
to come to their own point"*

       *

kitchen matches
or
   "Swans"
          will start
  the day the
morning

unbuilding the ac-
cumulated hearth,

unreflecting moon-
cinders,
ashes to be
carried out
every ritual
every Wednesday

on our foreheads,

        moonash / cold sperm
come
    that is gone already
        not moving her-ward,
male-cycle, night-cycle

    & mornings
    kitchen the first place
    against
the clouds banking the stars.

light hides . runs lightly to
its hearth
          the burrow that is the hearth
  of the process, crucible
  leading back to the furnace
  I was taught to bank
  at nightfall.

Swan song (first song
into day
& at half past time
out of fire

I run into the sun
-lit outside the afternoon
street leads to the store

& buy a bottle
of Spanish wine
the colour of blood
or fire & fags &
a box of safety

matches

HOUSEHOLD SHIP

made in Norseland
norwegian wood
matches
swedish sulphur

household light
tame fire waiting
for the wine
cooling in the ice box

    lights a different
    space

          *

                (evening, now, around, the, fire
how do we get
      to the bone
   of the matter within
without
       cutting the flesh
spilling the blood   spreading
          pain
     without & within . how do we
track the narrow path
leads to the marrow

   we stare into the fire

      furry flame   whirling   dervish
dance of matter
how many dancers
on a pin
through the brain the grey
matter of dawn
leads to the spine
sympathetic torque awhirl

    petrified knowledges
    our forefathers the Incas'
    forefathers practised
    trepanation

a scar-alphabet spelling secret
      spilling sacred
    runes of pain —

                    then hair growth
            hides the past or the
car accident, the mad dance, the cracking
                boulders, the falling
                    trees...

the future entangled in our hair

        we will not speak of grass or earth

                these matters require
                    discourse that more than verges
on the political.

                the context is access
        the text the right
of way
            the open lay
        of the land
                as the wolf pack closes in
el lobo sniffs the roots
of your hair
pisses on the flames
of your hearth
                    the moon is his excuse
                        dampen the spirits
                            of those lunatics
                (does not, wants not, to see that
                    the moon is
                        male

                        his projection
as el lobo the lunatic takes revenge
makes the women bleed
& beats their faces
to a bloody pulp
when they do not let him

fuck them in their / his
unclean state.

    *

      The State is run
     by such confusions.
       Is run over by
every wolf
can lift a leg
pisses on the light
burns at the heart of
the city
  /
    the fold is trampled he'll
   tear off the leg
     of any lamb
 or his own,
     the predator teeth
    fake glimmer,
     Irrlicht
reflects the trumped up
image, the ice-age, the dare-
win-ian technicoloured
opinion of
the age of our ancestors, their place
   the Pleistocene
    lied about
& to. & thus

we watch on the 24" screen
the stone age
  reduced to the dimensions of
 a cute curtsy-
ing dance for the queen
of this so-called commonwealth.

                while on the radio   the music
           of the spheres   on modulated frequency
boils down to   a 'news' bulletin
about the lady holds
the world record
for the loudest scream   (110 decibels; Concorde
               taking off emits 115...)

                        *

       all this, as they say, in a day's work
    at the end of which
        - day -, not the end
               of the work, or the world -
we are reduped
seduced, re
duced.

    *

*the correspondences of natural things with spiritual
things, or of the world with heaven, is through uses,
and uses are what conjoin.*

    *

*I read too much
to have any idea / of what I know*

    *

time now
time for a jorum for joris
sends me off again
blows against the empire
here a question of wine
the art of making it

seems lost when you
have to freeze all taste
to drink it.

      this is a loss of fire
or force, the strength
that lies at the root
of anything, or plant,
or act, well done.

      what's wrong with
the consumer
          is not that he does
consume, is that he has lost
   the care of discrimination
that he will eat
shit
   if ordered (or not)
  to do so.
      this is the matter
of enstasy.

      *

we will use this wine
to cook with,
      the slow fire
will dispel
the bad spirits,
      the good meat
is stronger than
the bad art.

on the hearth
the cook deals
with the problem

can only be
solved

        with alchemical
care: *how to
manage the heat* (G.L.)

    air, the flow
of air can spoil
the process
or else dispel
the noxious
spirits ex-
pelled from
the wine.

        it is not a matter
    of chance
           though
        chance be matter
enough
to enter

the process . stew
in your own juices .

you are caught
by the falling

night . you are
saved & thank the

tree
holds

the leather bag
your tent

up . against the falling
of the night . the shooting

star
signals

the meal
is ready

eat
me.

     *

You eat, your
night has fallen

now you fasten
the flapping

tentflap against
the voices whose

wet breath makes
the fire shiver.

El Lobo grimly
(Grimmbart)

tries again
to fool the fox.

you take off
the pelt, naked

you notice how
you marvel

how once again
you have moved

into the relative
safety of the two.

a man & a
woman by

the fire, the
place they

are. The three
are here but

the four are
far, so far

they are no
longer there.

*

(evening prayer:

    agnus dei
    agnus dei
    agnus dei

    ignis diei
    ignis diei
    ignis diei

*

    the common shore : the inside
           ledge where the sea
of fire   the fire
      floods
     against the ring
            of brick

      *

to say it clear
to sing connections
out of my madness
to make a dance-floor
for all our marriages.

      *

          an open fire
          the condition of trust

       love in the air
       fire on the hearth

      *

at the end of the day a tunnel

a red light its eye
the hearth shine
is not fox-fire
keeps alert watch
over the night
invites into
its long safety
him who has
fed it by day :
no fear : there is no
back to this cave

(the appearances
are saved) at the heart
of this fire
we do not lose substance
we are not consumed
here in the quiet
glow we sum up our love
we summon our liquids
our spillings do not extinguish
that fire
(coagulating
elated
stars
now here
there
at the heart
of our matters
we sleep
and our dreams
are the dance of the flames
tracing the secret knowledge
we will forget at dawn
and rediscover as we trace
our dance through the day

*

(morning prayer

O that Now, *nel mezzo* of my birthplace I arise

Having shared laziness, there is no time to waste

May I choose the undivided path of

    Listening, Reflecting & Meditating

So that, being born,

My time may not be squandered.

*

                    (noon   .   tracing the story

indication		
mathesis	p r e t e x t	idea of distinction
		contour
poem	t e x t	a universe
topology	c o n t e x t	the world

*

a universe is born
when a space is severed

by tracing the way
we represent
such a severance

we begin

to reconstruct
accurate coverage

the basic forms
underlying

we begin to see

the familiar laws
of our own experience

how

in
ex
ora
bly

they follow
from the original

act
of

severance

                        *

                  from any hearth
rises the whole
picture
    /
      transcendence
from the captive
to the new
(hitherto
unapparent)

vision beyond it.
beyond the severance
before the eye, in
front of, a
head

        the end of present existence's
        charts,
                the maps the rolls
        burned on the relative hearth
        heating the sealed alembic

        pressure cooker turning
        inside
        out

        the distances of time.

emit a picture
image made new
visible
viable

        the realisation of form

        that place cradles
        the way
we talk
& go

about our common life.

                take therefore
                the form of
                distinction

for the form

it's the 'same' sends us
to sleep, we will thrive
on difference, perfect
continence.

        the calling of the name
        is the value of the content

that, is, to, say,
            for any name,
                    to call is to recall.

to recall is to call.
& memory of difference
the intuition & instruction
to cross the boundary.

Draw the universe!

(you sit facing the fire
crossing your legs
uncrossing your legs)

in one turn
it makes
its appearance

particular only
in the price we pay
for its visibility.

                *

THUS THE STORY
thus the universe, thus, any turn
at the number four
in the possibilities of
movement the many
fold & twist this
tongue,
        thus the antlered

tongue, here, & by the fire
& in Cathay's
Bar des Anges Noirs
where when the emperor's
footprint's turned
to ice, the Four
Riders of the Logocalypse
run the show. Then
the DNA Kid spins his meta-
bolic roulette, scarlet
snowstorm, bleeding
runes tell a story cuts
deeper than, carves
the entangled letters
of a new genetic code
into the hard wood
of the tables. & *Frater G.*
a Saturnian secret
agent masquerading as the
Queen's own good Doktor
Dee, makes it turn
& stop at the double
four.
  Tonight
I sit by the fire
my glass
I sit & sip
my glass is full.

  *

This is more
than any
one or all
verses, I

argue with the silver-
smith,
           clarifying
the air, I show
the old man
show the process
of pruning count
the whole constellation
of words,
           getting it right

finally getting
there, the tired
sons of the old man
hand-struck creatures
who took from the all
all the manifest
& throw it in
with all the verses
           throw
it on the stone
circling
           &
                centring
the old man,
the world
was born & fired
in the hearth.

           *

           Four I say, Four; Four is the First Number,
           & from four you start
           you count

in any
direction.

*

>	simply
>	*bearing in mind*
>	what it is
>	one needs
>	to know

*

as they head out of
the sun
towards the fourth
planet.

    But the red
VW bus breaks down
slightly south
of the Microcosm
what some will call
the Inside-Whirl
a place a far
cry from the city
limits of "Welcome,
Unincorporated, North'
Carolina."

"Oh no, not another
Odyssey!" I say,
knowing better
& unpack
right here and

left there under
our eyes, the famous
Carbo-Astro-Scope,
whose four-directional
valences point
the way home & get us there
in the half-life
of an epic.

It was the history
I dreamed
this night
staring into the fire.

*

"We shall lose it all if it be not those voices talking over the evening fire. But the voices are gone. The waves throwing themselves down in ranks upon the shore are what I hear."

*

                                                (sol in cancer

4 a.m.

blue light above

dawn unbroken

at the edge of

where work has

brought me

breaking

the first birds

break

into song

as the sun

rising breaks

out of the ocean

breaks the

cracks his

claws

*

in a shut room
snow over the windows,
the hearth stoked, incandescent —

*

Day of pairing, of parting
my life
in the middle, & the longest
day of the year

already
was.
      How to manage
the losses
in night's short lap.
        (how to manage
the fire : keep it
in the open,
          the condition of,
trust.

       Her wing has grown
back of me, of my back,
a desire for silence.

I defy the walls that stand
revealed. Their bright
         /
           white
silence foreshadows
the unfolding of a fresher
universe.
        One verse closes, coming
closer to
making a world.

        *

"the hearth is not the world,
it is a universe."

       * * *

10 A.M.

to learn it by
doing it

the work
of morning

song of each
man &

morning the first
learning

the only ritual
not to avoid

sparrow song
chasing

the two
suns rise

& set
contrapuntally

the rising
but (no buts)

the imperfect
metaphor

but the lumen
osity

we hope
for

where sun
comes in

shadows
grow

here the morning
star no longer

casts a shadow
here you

rely on
a sign

in which
sun & moon

hold together
beyond Mazda

the lightbulb
to my left

(that the shadow
the writing

hand throws
not fall

on the writing)
of no use now

sun breaks
clouds

out of the
right corner

of my
eye

I
switch

the light off
act of faith

the first one
of the day

on which all the
others depend

EVENING

The single is
what is

easily
known.

ANGUISH, A RIDDLE

That all the languages are borrowed
but how then do I count them
that do not belong to me
                      In the first
one I think in the second I sink
the third is my rhetoric &
the fourth my west &
wagon its wheel
at least traces these steps
in harmonies of tetradic modalities
before & after I sink

LOVE SONG

to language this love.
sparks flying off
the intertwined tongues.

sparks . turn to larks .
      laughter
         love

OUT OF THE DEEP...

out of the deep salt-end of the year

out of nebel cloud the bright coin

ascends, readying

      the rites of mid-winter

           hope arising

UNTITLED

The most complex act
we have to
inform our ongoing
to stave off the complicatedly
rigorous lies
of simplicity, is
in the fly's eye
the centre of the web
is a manifold dark & manifest

the threat of the thread
that binds the spider's ass
more irrevocably to the web
than the life of the fly

refracts in the breaking
of the nodal eye

THE ANGLE & THE DIRECTIONS

there is no vertical route
the voyage is via curve of surface
with & through the tension holds
the words in buoyant dance
the *etymon* the lie
lost continent at bottom of
where the sands no longer shift
what the hand made sent
only a root rooted
in itself ie nowhere
where only no-man could find her
the imaginary city of gold
past or future

the lie of the impossible present
the land's lay forgotten
sent to the bottom
for the sake of a dream
went to the sky went
too high went where there is
no air to breathe where
we cannot live
neither above so below
but in the middle
we are rooted along the multiple nodes
curve of her breast it is here
we the vertical ones link with
out perpendicular roots
the words.

MIDNIGHT IN CAMBRIDGE

Scotus Eregina,
the switch by the door
you'll have to go there
to turn it around
& switch darkness on
for sleep for
sleep
& the light of dream

SUNDAY MORNING POEM

on the yellow patterned sheets
in the plain beige light
downstairs you watch
tea making itself

wind moves between
the wall & the world—
map a coat of many colours
cools its heels & the first move
is ours is our
time & the wind
the wind makes room for the sheet-
lightning our bodies
turn to waves

SORE THUMB

in opposition
to the general hand

a gesture liable
to amputate

the gentle fist
will remedy
that arrogance

but the opposable thumb
made part of
the genetic description

may as yet help us
hitch a ride

will get us
where we need to go

in time to catch
the whole show

from TRACING

for Paige Mitchell

8/1/1975 1.30 p.m.

Up
finally . bitter
morning
         coffee
followed
by a glass
of
  Soave . cold
in mouth
wakes up
connections,
slight headache &
missing person
is
    EUROPA
my woman from
Tyre attends
the grapes
of all our directions.

    (there is no such
    thing as West)

& the Maya
had only two
such 'points' of
reference,
their sky
kept rushing
their
heads held back
thrown back
no stars fixed
      (mobility of every
         man & woman)
keeps rushing
nos ancêtres
les Gaulois
hold the same terror
same torque & twist
kept the sky for a while
it fell, broke
our necks not
our heads
a spiral
nebula groggy
foggy w/ mead
but wiser no
use in human
sacrifice
no gods fixed

enough stars
in this theatre
to be paid off
i.e. kept
from falling
      (all you kept gods
harlots of our
metaphysics

   (by & thru bribery
at the crossroads they
hold out a cap,
spare a dime?
or damn you
meester sapiens

or else?
a dime novel
where rushed by
the stagecoach
out of Mesilla
carries the Father
you'll kill
at the crossroads
you'll spill his white blood
don't spill our red blood
on altars of decapitated
knowledges, the hearts
twitch, empty
muscles, that
old god at the crossroads
nailed to what was
a spiral torque
once, now stilled
now arrested
by the local
sheriff
another father came
from another
state
took over the show
the whorehouses &
spinning wheels
the roulette tables
  fixed
    the double

cross / double
                    / zero
introduced (the house
        (always
(wins

nail the suckers
the son got nailed
the cross stood stead-
fast when the spin
stopped.
            laundered moneys
our heads filled
the grapes rushing
cool cold like &
unlike winter here
no afternoon
goddess
            EUROPA
tickles my spine
her swine
the altar ego
ergo shrine
nape & neck
in a car
in a vacant star or
stare,
            our lot

among men drunk
on fixed stars
out flat on a flat earth
an earth gone flat
(& not to seed)
like the wheel of the coach
fallen off the axle
the tree grows downward

lays us flat
on a flattened earth
see that sky
rushing us by &
above your shoulders
your head
sticks out
      beyond the crab
          nebula

   *

27/ II / 75

Earth
is altar
& what
we lay
upon her
goes up
any
number
of ways.
We can
lay
nothing
to rest.
But us.
We will rest
in her,
my dead
knees
under the table.
      Bones
of the saints
are necessary

ingredients,
I kiss
the stone,
the earth needs salt
in fire we will
give her salt
now bake a cake
mola salta, of spelt
& salt:
    she is the salt
of this earth, we need
not sacrifice
on this altar
we give
at the round
table in talk
with companions
knees touching
alive
do not taunt 'the merits
of Thy saints whose
   relics are here'
  buried
in earth where we
shall all be
saints . human
sacrifice
under or above
the table a
recent degradation.
No need
for that, it is
the talk we want, not
   the scream
    rises
     the steam
      rises

from the cut breast
      the heart ripped out
offered up, not given
  its resting place
     below
        so that
          what remains
(the congealed fibres)
      has to be eaten
(oh eat your hearts out,
         priests
    of the upper
reaches,

around this table
this altar as new as
the pleistocene
there are no priests
only celebrants
of the light
and the knees
touching spark
a light in dark
that we may see
our ancestors
the buried saints
for they are all saints
those who are dead
we call your names
& leave a place
you sit
with us around
this table.
         no such thing as
a *tabula rasa*
she is always already
there, always

already begun
before we even start.

    & on the table
we lay the bright
      /
        white
            ice-
sheet, we spread
   our time
      no obsidian knifes
for the honey of
our lives.

   (who hid the honey
in a jar?
   who slammed the door
on the door?
   who slapped a cup
over the cup,
     & a cross on top
does not open the grail?)

   mystery
  is about revealing
what is secret
can therefore
not remain thus.
Though at times
it may seem necessary
to hide
we never hide
not to be found.
   He who hides
for the sake of
hiding
burns a stolen heart

goes up in smoke
will never be
seen again.
    The E on
any stone
   is revealed by a kiss
     reveiled
   by a priest
   reviled
if displaced
   into hierarchy
     of darkness.

    6 / III / 75 2-3 p.m.

   the matter
     will not rest.
& the gift
   the permission
to begin anywhere.
   Take it
   from there.
Anywhere . Anyplace
   place
   enough to
   turn
     on.
To shed
further light
on that old matter
futhark
a trace in matter
but, but father
I tell you
no longer (in the present

dispensation)
arche
(tho arc
remain, we'll keep
the buildings, cool
shade under arcades
to stroll & discourse
with friends in
Sevilla or Cordoba.

Where I'll contend
that with *arche*
gone there is
no need for
telos either
way.
(tho tellus
remain,
a future
resting place
we know now).

But this is not the future,
this now
is not the past either
though it contain
more
than the time-
worn trinity.
A whole that
is more than,
a common-place
by now,
now & uninteresting
per se, as it is only
per others
by penetration either

way, what is called
            the crossing
       of borders
that it touches
me to move.
            Through the holes
in the whole light
enters, begs
our eyes,
            carries
the voices,
            the voices riding
home on the lightbeams.
We are luminous
beings
& the waves
ride us both ways
& the particles
the digital mode
our most
dangerous ally.

Take it from here,
take it from
anywhere but don't
take it
from me. I'll
give it to you
anyway I can.
            The way
it was given
to me.
Or the way
given me
to give.

      Some of it
given by a sweet
lake. I was
rowing that
boat when
Jean-Jacques
leaned over,
put a halt
to my frantic
action & said:
      "There are
those who gravely
give us
for philosophy
the dreams
of a few bad nights.
      Now
you may say
that I too dream -
I agree -
      but whereas
those others
take no heed,
I give my dreams
as dreams
letting those
who are awake
search them for
what may be
of use."

      But I am
weary of Frenchmen
as of literary
dreams.
      A dream
is, as this now,

its own inter-
pretation.
    & I wake
to write
as I woke to talk
the sense of
rainfall.
    Or did it
talk me? Not
here a question of
the other, we'll
leave that angle
for the time
being, or for
a rainier
day, probably
in France & more
likely than not
in the past.

    What I mean
is that the first
obedience is to
what is said.
To hear it.
To hear is to heal
& in the patter of rain
is written
(I hear it)
the dream of the new
language, needed
if we are to go on.
Not out, not in
we need to go
on to that place
where to hear
is to speak

are not separate
activities, separate
modes labelled
one the passive
& the other the active.
This new language
arises not from
an already formed
speech but out
of the very necessity
of speech.
        Thus a
Glossopoeisis
(Artaud so accurate
on these matters)
a language
neither imitative
- mimesis, the Greek
said, making monkeys
out of us for too long -
nor a creation
of names
        but a movement
leads us back
to the edge
of the moment
when word is not
born yet, a place
where articulation
though already
no longer scream
is not yet discourse,
where repetition
is nearly impossible
& with it,
language.

17 / III / 75   10.30 pm

what we are
left with
is what leaves us,
tracks in the snow
the thought
through the brain,
this book
called *Tracing*,
the act of
to write
a meditation
leaves me
a trace
the only other
we have
or can.
Always outside
as every act is
where each thought
is as it moves
through the brain
across the varied
fields of all
our landscapes.

(It is slow work
today, plodding
my way
through that snowdrift
of thought man
has banked up
against himself
ever since

the true ice melted
leaving him
on the vast plains
of an unexpected
earth,
a malleable substance
- he thought -
& with the oxen
of his will
yoked to
the gleaming
ploughshare his
fumbling had
forged,
      he begun
to describe
the economy
of his life.)

A metaphor
for writing?
A meat for
image, amphora
full of some
kind of eternity?
No,
      no need for it,
anyone who has
a body may find
the implicit
sulcate heart.
A lover will
point to it
for the blind
one, finger-
wise.
      & track it

from the margin
of the spinal cord
where Kundalini
sleeps coiled ad-
jacent to the central
median fissure,
via the shallow
groove on the outside
of the heart's right
atrium to the fissured
map of the brain.
     From where
we all speak
with forked
tongues, for the *sulcus
terminalis* the final
fissure is the V-shaped
groove gives
the ratio of the tongue.
Two thirds out front
& loose
the last third anchored
further back.

     It is
from our bodies's
furrows that the first
permission arises.
The drag of it. The pull
of the pen across
the magic writing pad.
It is the necessary
violence we all call
life,
     & see now
as what it, no,
not as what it is,

but does, that fact:
death's economy.
We know the process
it is us, we cannot
stop it as we
cannot stop us.
      Towards the end
of his life, Freud
still stuck but
closer to it,
closer:

"When writing, which consists in making a liquid flow from a pen upon a sheet of white paper, has taken on the symbolic significance of coitus, or when to walk has become the substitute of the trampling of the body of the earth-mother, then both writing and walking are abandoned, because they would be that acting out of the forbidden sexual act."

But the syntax is wrong.
The articulation.
We keep walking, keep
writing from the beginning
on, is the essential
act of our self-
creation. Via
(always (already
rupta.
      No other way
to go.
What Artaud called
the cruel
meaning
necessary

law, *la loi
de la maison,*
first organisation
of an inhabitable
space where we
may know our
selves as he did:
"*Moi, Antonin
Artaud, je suis
mon fils,
mon père,
ma mère,
et moi.*"

    But the oxen
grow tired, the sickle
of the moon has traced
a long furrow thru
this night, the will
of the instrumental
oxen tempts the
tired hand,
refusing obedience
to the crooked lay
of the land under-
hand would like
to go the easy
path, the straight
line I have to
fight knowing
it is the poem
I want, that map
true to the crookedness
underfoot, & must
refuse philosophy I know
to be the
lazy ploughing,

the diachronic map.
The history of
philosophy
is the world becoming
prose. Before Plato
even, there lived
a man
called Pherecydis
on the island of Scyros
who we are told
"was the first
man to write in
prose."
    & Condillac
to muse: *Finally*
a philosopher
unable to bend himself
to the rules of poetry
began to write
in prose!
    The easy
continuity. The lure of
eternity. The image
of absolute possibility.
The bait that hooked
the tired oxen. The moon
sickle out of sight now.
You already asleep.
To join you not
at the end
of this thought
but from its in-
ception on.
    Your silent
call whispering what
that Murcian
"the son of a small saw"

chiselled
out of words, free
of arabesques, a straight
reminder, notch
in the tree of life,
whispering, whispering
that the heart
is capable
of every form:
"Love is the creed
I hold wherever
turn his camels,
love is still
my creed & faith."

Let it be.
Enough.
I am coming.
To you. There.
Here. Where
I am. Where
you are. Here
I am you are
(not as
(but one
or a
trace or track
love has dreamed
tonight.

BRECCIA

1.
agglomerate deposit
sharp fragments
a fine-grained matrix

2.
the minute & the very large
but mainly the figure arose
between these two

3.
from under rock
where the old appetites walk
& I talk out of Homer

4.
shoulderblade cracked in heat
a map of fissures
the art of writing

5.
we'll make it
by the skin
of our teeth

6.
riparian dawn
things to be picked up
to be toyed with & tried

7.
(out of Homer the stem
is strong repose:
to lie still & keep still

8.
as O under the ram's belly
evading the fathers
"lie quiet Ez, this is Chas speaking"

9.
cubo : to lie asleep, also sexual
& death - fr. root to bend (so elbow
& concubine, & in English hump hoop hip heap

10.
the fleece now
in the fullness of earth
you found old honey

11.
pushed a flower up by its root
we are at the beginning
another age, yucca-age

12.
appropriating in relation to nature
expropriating in relation to man
poverty a relation between people

13.
the blatant vulgarity
of a pseudo-scientific language
preoccupied with warfare

14.
from the large grass-eaters
pelvic bones
a sort of natural drinking cup

15.
at best a night's lodging
not bedrock
open-eyed, we rest like hares

16.
learning the language of being alive
organs & functions
activity of the hands

17.
"We are ready to admit
anything - except
to have begun at the feet"

18.
carapaces of turtles
tough strands of beach vine & kelp
driftwood seasoned in salt water

19.
needs of iodine & salt
benefits from unsaturated fats
inclination to high protein intake

MAHLER'S QUINCUNX

in memory of Anick Joris

1.

    ex-
pressed be-
reavement   dour

Trauer it was
not that most normal pitch
instrument in the shape of
mouth   in the hollow of the mouth
pitch of the sound

-ed mouth   vowel
scale of far-off bird flight
black ticked-off name
of dead one the six
vowels make a V
tongue's back part raised
& a progressive protruding of the lips

lops the dream words off in
midair

2.

       a stick through the sun
       or thorn in the eye?
       the Phoenicians monkey
       ing around or
       moon-

key a thin finger
on the moon
cuts early time
span before children
move into sun-
cycle . died at dead
of night
white wet slime
their bodies newts still
under that moon
dead still now husk
Kind

        Lilith is coming
        Lilith is here

3.

: muted   velar
stops . when your
luck runs out

into the night
your shadow
doesn't find

its way back
dazzled by a sun
it has never seen

it turns to dew
drops .   stops

She laps up
a curse for
thirst   .

                    I do not
mean tears

4.

rips . the cord
                rips
                        no bell so
        who can tell
        whose an outer
                whose an inner
life . no measure but
that ripped chord
        highest pitch
dot in the eye
        takes over
cord looked at
    transversally
        a sighting
        along a tunnel
that is death's
        itch

5.

messy brass apotheosis
the complexity of
life under death
life after life
under fire of
will   that is
movement   & no
stopping it

that cry does not stick

in the throat
sticks through the sun
one-eyed   cross-eyed
we all   the scream
balances
in the throat
the voice breaks
that stick in
two now half
flies out
a bee half
trickles down
honey of life
gorge your
self can
bridge in song

end of song.

THE BOOK OF LUAP NALEC

para mis Europeos
para mis muertos

We will never look very good
We are too far gone on thought, and its rejections
The two actions of a Noos

Edward Dorn

Artistik ist der Versuch der Kunst, innerhalb des allgemeinen Verfalls der Inhalte sich selbst als Inhalt zu erleben und aus diesem Erlebnis einen neuen Stil zu bilden, es ist der Versuch, gegen den allgemeinen Nihilismus der Werte eine neue Transzendenz zu setzen: die Transzendenz der schöpferischen Lust..

... im Grunde also meine ich, es gibt keinen anderen Gegenstand für die Lyrik als den Lyriker selbst.

Gottfried Benn

THE BIRTH OF LUAP NALEC

(...)

somewhere a door closes.
I am not awake
alone . I am

thinking of
you, lady
la nuit américaine
I'm thinking

the strong body of America arched
night over an ephectic Europe

'e n t r o p o c e p h a l u s'

God's peace, Benn, would have that coin
(age that knew the brain's skin
Roman des Phänotyp:
played Doktor
wrote Morgue
dies)

Celan dares
go further, *Faden*
sun through
threadbare
web,
his breath

turned

to water.

How dare you
dare?
  Face
myself
past the bright
wound mirror?
    Stare
where you
single counter-
swimmer
count
  &
   break
the floated
spines,
the lines.

  Time
broke us
in,
  saddled us
with a sadness
(post-modern, no,

post-mortem) its
vigour the rigor
of water now
frozen, the white
silenced sheet,
Pleistocene
place I search
to find
the shifted
stance.

Sight threads sense shreds
from the folded image knit

behind time:
        invisible enough
to see you, you came
through all the walls
you came turncoat eye

eye turned
inside out
of which
I see

Scintillation of
my she break
the thin
film
    the ice-white
skin
    an angled slit
reverses where
we were.
      are.
        From where
       (here & there)

SPRECHGITTER

I
the shifter, am spoken
through
these chambers -
a quartering
of words
    badly bruised
    & water-logged
but I must keep
on talking keep
calling

your name
changeling, maiden

what is
your name
what is it
shimmers, stammers
on the vocal-cords-bridge, in the
Great Inbetween
with all that has room in it
even without speech?

Antara   you call

yourself there
Lady of the Gate
& here
       Gate
of the Lady
         through
which Nalec
lately hither-
silenced,
alived
despite all
by the breath of
the shifting ice.

Out of a dream of drowning
the drowning,
of a dream the contra-
script
read us into meeting
in the Serpentcoach
takes us
       once past
your white cypress

through the cypher-
wall.

      Thus break the ice
to know.
Though we had met
before it had been
I
in you
from birthseed
out, til now when
I in you
is
Nalec
whom open
you enter
now through him
at last
      you climb
in me
up the dark
memory shaft
        you climb
to the day.

Light entered me
lit the walls
of the cave
I was. A fistful
of consonants
drifts from mouth to
mouth, in-
ward
      the lightbeams
dance them
wall-
      word where

the vowels wait
obedient to the light
where
syllable by syllable
the loud heartthread
is trembled
clear.
        Your voice
Antara
declares itself -
I begin
to witness
at the end

of a long day

done . done . done .

AFTER DONE TRYING TO WAKE HER UP

merciless

we go by
sound alone.

bark back:
at the end
was the word.

He said it is done.

Thrice reaped
the long day's
echo
    /ing
       . done .
           in)

&
Luap Nalec
rose, stood
against the end.
We no longer go by
but stay, cowering
erring
      haunched

nostrils flare for
the reaped echo's
shell turns
to earth.

the earth turns
to mire
    && mirth
        && myrrh.

ends smell
of dung, of
things done in

thus now the newly
sounded smells stir
the small grey earths
make possible:

        matters like take
        a tree's dead trunk
        a word to be dug out
        a will comes in
        we fire-hollow
        the vowelled belly
        then sand the ends
        arched consonants
        down to firm
        mirror-roundness

Roll on . From here
uphill. Go. OVERland. OVERnight. Nearby. Here
HEAR space beckons now the boats now the place beckons
the readymade the signed objects / singed subject this old
construct continent renamed renamable.

        Singing the singed parts.

The burned offerings
up up in flames
putrify the hard chains
purify the heart claims.

A wide-on she says I have a wide-on for Europe
I am she & you singer I have a soft spot for you
Antara make me fucker give me rope
enough to know your face the whole
length I'll sing it now

        :
        that the links be made
        visible again
        I'll weave a meshless
        net of space
        you are the song
        are the loom
        I am the breath
        turns & spins
        the yarn
        anew.

HYMEN: I) fr. GK *hymen* wedding song, fr. *Hymen* God
of marriage
(lit. a wedding cry); perhaps akin to GK *hymnos* hymn,
song of praise.
1) *archaic* : marriage
2) *archaic* : a wedding song

II) fr. GK *hymen* membrane, caul (perhaps akin to SK *syuman* band, thong):
a fold of mucous membrane partly closing the orifice of the vagina.

SYU-:   To bind, sew.
Variant form *su-*; OE *seam* seam.
Suffixed from *su-tro-*: in SK *sutra,* thread, string.
Suffixed shortened from *su-men* : in GK *hymen* thin skin   membrane.

Das Gedicht behauptet sich am Rande seiner selbst; es ruft und holt sich, um bestehen zu können, unausgesetzt aus seinem Schon-nicht- mehr in sein Immer-noch zurück.
Paul Celan

La scène n'illustre que l'idée, pas une action effective, dans un hymen (d'où procède le rêve), vicieux mais sacré, entre le désir et l'accomplissement, la perpétration et son souvenir: ici devançant, là remémorant, au futur, au passé, sous une apparence fausse de présent. *Tel opère le Mime, dont le jeu se borne à une allusion perpétuelle sans briser la glace: il installe, ainsi, un milieu pur, de fiction.*

Stéphane Mallarmé

Mal tu par l'encre même
                Stéphane Mallarmé

Et me détacher de l'idée de l'être est-ce en faire un ou se tenir toujours en dehors? Je crois que c'est se tenir en dehors dedans, en y étant, et y être ce n'est pas se tenir au-dessus du Mal mais *dedans* et être le Mal lui-même, le Mal qu'il y ait Dieu à rassasier, l'hymen de la Morgue qui est que le pli ne fut jamais un pli...

        Antonin Artaud

TYMPAN: 1a: drum
        b: a celtic bowed stringed musical instrument

      2a: (obs.) TYMPANUM
      b: any of various membranous plates functioning basically   like the membranous tympanum of the ear.

       3a: *or* TYMPAN SHEET: a sheet of material (as paper or cloth) in a printing press that is placed between the impression surface and the paper to be printed.

TYMPANUM: The tense double membrane separating the outer from the middle ear - tympanic membrane - called also eardrum.
     A membrane in a sound producing organ that acts as a resonator.

TYMPANIC NERVE: a branch of the glossopharyngeal nerve arising from the petrosal ganglion, distributed to the walls of the tympanum of the ear where it takes part in forming a plexus.

THE NEWT LIFE

> *Mas per melhs assire*
> *mon chan,*
> *vau cercan*
> *bos motz en fre*
> *que son tuir cargat e ple*
> *d'us estranhs sens naturals;*
> *mas no sabon tuich de cals.*
>
> Guiraut de Bornelh

Dee-doo, dee-dum.

No such thing
as a simple twist

Dee-da, dee-doo,
"What is it stammers
under the lintels of words

a breath of air"
Dee . Die .
       Die Dame Art
Amiss
    echoes of
hilaritas
(common salt
added to
the rarer gold
of *cars rimas*)
& never sad
thus spoke
the shuffled
words of cause.

  Re : birth
breath-sound
of the sun
coming
in the maiden.

   (the given
Doors
  tympan & hymen
oblique boundaries
of sound
  &,
   hammer-
headedness) the

"asunderwritten"
on the made bed
of fall or
fall's ore
  (gold) aurora
l'aura,
  autumn's *Atem* a
  breath
  breaking
on the unmade bed
  through
  taking
summer's hymn, her
maiden:
  had . done for .
  taking
it all in
to
 where
a newt life beckons.

Sap.
    Filling the gaps
my hollowed teeth & I
the cranky lion.
Lie low, sweet form.

Come again, come
fill her, ful-
fill the prostrate
prophecy.
        A
proffered apple that
won't bite
you who are
at this late twist re-
turned
from rust
to lust
      (a verb
to dare win/ter
: thrice strapped
to the must
you miss
the music our
lion's share.

     Miss
the false air, *l'aura*
of pestilence,
etiological clouds
to be seeded
in a different
city.

Dee-doo, dee-dum,
no such thing
as a simple twist.

      In the middle
of the newt life
      winter
won over
time now time
enough to
choose & leave
a language
where
      "verb"
is a noun &
eye means
verge
      or urge
      a verge
cannot come
to mean.

THE EAR

Strapped & sealed
he missed the music.
The spoils

for greed of which
the crew goes overboard
harvests nothing
but the languish of fishes.
Fool's gold
lure of *Muspelheim,*
shiny coin your
face rubbed out rubbed
down to the blank
stare of the sea's
surface.

While the stultified
ship shuttles on
we follow its course
with eyes strained
no line links it
to a loom it drifts
with masts sung earthward
set free in a space
where right side up
& upside down
no longer mean
it weaves along
not ship not church
a shapeless shape.

Protected
by his hymened
tympanum
no longer

divided
in his attentions
- impregnable fortress -
the lion
listens,
        hears
the gyroscope
the only function
of his organ.

Strapped
to his stirrups
he swings
a hammer sounding
the walls.
        Follows
the echo's
threads &
careful not to
lean against
the shaky ramps
begins to explore
the beginnings of
his story.

    Tympanum . Labyrinth . Hymen . Thread .

Advancing now
(standing
      walking
           dancing)
wrapped into
he moves
enveloped never
to emerge again
the form of an ear
built around a dam

turning about
its internal wall.

Newt shape
of a city
he feels along
(a labyrinth
semi-circular canals
- semi-lunar)
         a city
wrapped
like a snail
around a floodgate
a dam
      stretching
towards the sea, closed
in upon itself
but open towards
the sea.

      Amazed
the lion finds
himself
on a beach
he bends down
to the other form
the female form
picks up
what the sea
spelled out a
shell
      full &
emptied of its
waters
        anamnesis
of the sea's ear
the only sound

    against
his ear.

       It happens
has to happen
here . the crack
resounds
      birth
of a language
a different song
"sexual jubilation
is a glottal choice of
a lunar canal
the clear auricular ringing
a clear instillation of
sound"

      cracks
the wax seal
cuts the straps
     release
& the storm
abides.

MATROSEN LIED

> *(Infamous Baines, that early supergrass,*
> *testified that Christopher Marlowe held*
> "That all they that loue not
> Tobacco & Boies were Fooles...")

        How
the rising sun
thru these curtains
goes at me
again & again
mid-mornings
falls across my desk
how it sprawls
over the notebook how
it gains heat from
my coffee growing cold.

        How
leaning back I light a cigarette
admiring the four-coloured
sailor on the blue-white pack.
HERO it says on his cap
a bearded hero's head
between sail & steam
surrounded not by sea
but by a life buoy.
Look alive boy,
your cheeks are pink
your lips are red
your beard the colour
of tobacco
& you look serious
sternly boyish
in your light blue sailor shirt

       Was it he
helped Thomas Harriot
carry his cases ashore?
His 19C look does not deceive
he's immeasurably older
it is he who as a old man
taught young Ralegh how to use
the astrolabe, & he
knows the spot
where Drake lies buried.
He lashed Ulysses to the mast
& did the same for Turner
shaking his head, wondering
at the foolishness of men:
it's not the kind of thing
he'd do, he knows better
has lived longer & is
satisfied with his quart of rum
a day.

       Below deck
while the storm rages
& the sirens sing
he sips his drink
reflecting on how
doing the necessary
should be enough
for any man
immensely man
he sits among his mates
satisfied that he is immortal
because of the casual accuracy
with which he fulfils
the necessary confronting him.
For him no need for siren song
though it will be a tall tale to tell
in the taverns between now & then.

If I were a man
who still fell in love with sailors
I would surely fall in love with him.
I'd love him in all the narrow beds
from Brest to Valparaiso
we would armwrestle in Hamburg's *Kneipen*
down *copas* of *sangre de toro*
in the bodegas in Barcelona
one hand caressing his sleeping head
resting on my knees one hand
drawing love-tattoos in the wine-spill
on the wooden tables older
than age. O how I'd worship
his arched cock
his perfect balls!

    Unsung hero
let me sing you
suck you
off this packet of cigarettes
the smoke I exhale
curls in the air
folds in sunlight
tornado, typhoon
or simple tempest
I peer deeply into
your left glass eye
(you left the good one
in a brothel in Shanghai
as payment for the favours
of a mongolian princess)
I see a storm
& a shipwreck
off the Scillies
I watch you swim ashore
clutching the black Aztec mirror
between your teeth

it's all you're left with
you owe it your life
or that's what you think
& two weeks later
you barter it in a tavern
near Deptford for the charms
of a boy once laid
with Marlowe.

    The sun
is higher now
we dream in time
the time it took
to write this down
or the time it takes
the sun to dry
this ink.
The coffee's
quite cold now
sweet & gold now
as cold as last night's dream
when I threw down the bedside lamp.
I forgot the dream
& now wonder
did I dream of the sun
falling or of
a ship going down
of a face heated & reddened
by the sun at sea?
How come this morning -
what was it this morning -
made me look at the daily
packet of Players
was it what the dream
wanted or was it
what made me
dream?

TANITH FLIES

What has he to say?
In hell it is not easy
to know the traceries, the markings

Charles Olson

Desire, denied.
A man running
in his dream.
The nine lives
hit, a strike
on the alley
& the kingpin
lost three
left them stuck
in the three holes
of the crystal ball.

*

A bell. So this is hell's
kitchen. A rope tied to an invisible
spark. A shark. I hand it
to you in the living room
which isn't heaven either.

The tv has eaten all our meals
& now we eat it. Or is it.
difficult to say.
The rhymes rebound on the molten snow.
The sky is in the head.
The head is in the oven.
The oven is in the kitchen.
The kitchen is to the left of the living room

depending on where you stand.

*

it comes pouring in
your dayliness

the edge we are
trounced upon

doors opening &
intermittant

rain.

*

the full moon & the red moon
my stare & mood, your round dance
in the dream walking through fog
a pitchblack night, sticky sheets
I wake up with the sun high in
the sky in the room; the women
in my dream, unknown even there,
recede & vanish here. The ritual
of coffee making, decomposition

of movement into its smallest parts,
the daily repetition, against myth,
the first foothold of the day.
I love you. The women are gone
now, resorbed by your eyes.

I want to ask you how come
the other night in bed
my manifest & hard desire
did not wake you?
      What
were you dreaming
& by what means
could I have climbed
into your dream
made love to you there?
Loving each other it must
be possible to confoutre
our dreams & wakings
your dream my waking your
waking my dream?

   *

our obsessions or
my deer & foxes

    a way to see through
    the opaqueness of our selves

    a way to look at
    the transparency of the world

to make it (us) hold
more than water

though we will never be rid
of that confusion

      *

I beg to differ.
He bags a difference.
The public, the third person singular
the political & the social
thrive on identity.

              Seeing our
selves sleep we fall asleep.
Dreaming that you are
asleep I wake up
in my dream
sleeping next to you.

      *

in the back room
the kittens play
with my quartered body
the languages

pull timeward

ebb & flow &

inbetween froze

the windrose

at night
white wandered around

erasing the names of places
— an old alphabet was
banned — it became
difficult to find our way
as we drove at the night

*

last night we stalked the sky
then came in from the cold
into where our asteroid thoughts
flared & emptied
into bodies speech had hollowed
to lie there - blind dice
in a bottomless grail - unplayable
slagheap that slowly sinks us
into sleep,
    whirls us through faded silent
rushes of december dreams
    here, holding each other
we separate, fall
  through different sprockets,
       wake
astounded.

*

. but my cats . Something preceded something followed though we never know will never know how we got there. But. Caught claw in the leather strap of the briefcase. Or habit. We live somewhere, then pull back. Astonished we watch the furthest extension of our body hooked into the other matters. Matter. Wow! How did I get here, there, I mean, how... Lunge forward, new words, trouble spelling, caught & released claws. To approximate (asymptote!) an accuracy of love. That was before. Elsewhere & here in

Africa a chair of palm leaf spines & a red berber rug & a different red that is the same plus sun & white lozenges & Max's scream a lozenge too. The double-edged sword of self-consciousness. & then you come & it's you & I & two cats & this is Africa.

   *

  sea urchin thoughts
  lazy roll along ocean floor
  here every way is
  a possible direction
     starcraft
  or cosmological practice
  - not theory -
     or burden

  the music remains
  outside
  in here we fumble
  trying out silences
  we mistake for rhythm.

  a violin
  played
  the way the arabs do

  between the legs.
  how do we know
  that we don't.

  the short hairs
  string the bow
  the resin
    love's residue
  makes no sound.

   *

to wear veils
to make the eyes
visible
   forced
to do their doing

look at the music

falls down
the spiral staircase
in the Grand Mansion ear
doesn't reach
the mansarde in Paris

Monk sounds
a blue eiderdown
a white sheet
shaken out
a window

mask of a mask
see-through veils
all the way down
to the ankles

   *

lined & empty space
terror as usual
sleep or no sleep
the flies & their lord
darken the window
the cries of the black cat
I can do nothing for
not even silence
not even silence
to stand on

the flies inside now
the fate of the first born
in the sign of Tanith
a clay pot in a
hollowed stone
grey ash &
flies crawl along
the curve of moon
the sun is dotted
in her centre
wound-eye
stormed
by the black
armies the
sowers of night
sowers of salt
every child
is terrible
out of it
an adult horror
sleek hair
& a way with
the world
my angel
my sister
left Terra
buried in ice
the heat of
the sun could
not be stopped
fever sister
heat angel
holds a terror I
no longer
resemble

*

all night long
> the beacon of Cap de Garde
>> swept the stars out of the sky

all night long
> two dogs combed the beach
>> howling at the new moon

last night
> I saw the richest libra-sky ever
>> clouds this morning

a strong southern wind brings sand
> JP pours half a glass of cold water
>> into the coffee

> > > the grounds settle

> > > *

how the three of us, all
males, one
célibataire, one
expecting father, one
état marital,
> > last night in
the tv room
of the Hotel El Mountazar
were horny & angry
watching the pretty blonde english girl
hustling & being hustled
by the algerian cocksman
in the red polo shirt
the tight crotch hugging pants
how our jokey all-male banter
dried up

& our fantasies
stood visible
in the smoke filled
room, how
three separated spectres
settled like horns on our heads
& watching we sipped our coffees
caught in the net woven by
the dead talk of the unlaid.

*

the absoluteness of the moment
of fear or despair or simple
sadness,
   the fly squashed
against the light
transparency of the window
blood-smudge on an ordinary day's ritual
split-second death
   then I open the windows
let sun in, air,
flies.

house flies, horse flies, blue-bottles, winged
& buzzing moment
of my fear, a fear-fly
my body armed
a rolled-up newspaper
smash'em
forget the moment's futility
spontaneous inescapable creation
at the mountain of refuse
deep inside
an infinity of buzzing moments
take off

black squadrons
travel the day lazy
leading of my sky-space
they travel sure of their deaths
sure
the killing never ends
in despair a match lit
instantaneous spontaneous combustion
a dream mountain
the geology of my corpse
folded into their impervious
unreadable patterns

small fry hunter of
the rolled-up newspaper
I stalk the flies
a frenzy translated
into concentration

an early morning in Africa
the pen skids on the stain
left by the squashed fly-life
we make our spaces safe
& empty as usual
unable to live
with others

*

what we do not understand
sounds all the same to us

thursday night music of an arab wedding
& the dogs, the dogs bark in the night

even the instruments, unseen, cannot be understood
the voice, not understood, remains unseen

the watery ink into which I cast
the red-veined net of desperate waking

sad fish for seagulls' delight
my heart goes out, then down

swims towards an island of foreign sounds
worded in recurrence & all I know

is the abstract name of the ritual
being enacted, in this language, marriage.

a music I think of as yours -
not a question of property
but a presence & an intensity
one yields to
        as I do
to my thoughts of you so
distant, so near, in
this house this music as
all doubles I wonder
& wondering
soon I'll
        dare.

      *

the figs on the table
overripe
        explode
a shower of
fruitflies

life is spontaneous
creation in that sense
spontaneous putrefaction
out of which
we rise into our day

    *

a star tattoo
how simple it was
to see you
in that old berber woman
her forehead
shining through

    *

star woman
a dream etymology
with steps of light
you were all of them
& I woke
to berber drums.

from WRITING / READING

«... S'il y a une unité de la lecture et de l'écriture, comme on le pense facilement aujourd'hui, si la lecture est l'écriture, cette idée ne désigne ni la confusion indifférenciée ni l'identité de tout repos; le est qui accouple la lecture à l'écriture doit en découdre.

Il faudrait donc, d'un même geste, mais dédoublé, lire et écrire... Le supplément de lecture doit être rigoureusement prescrit par la nécessité d'un jeu, signe auquel il faut accorder le système de tous ses pouvoirs.»

Jacques Derrida, *La Dissémination*.

"... la poesia non nace da le regole, se non per leggerissimo accidente; ma le regole derivano da le poesie: et pero tanti son geni e specie de vere regole, quanti son geni et specie de veri poeti."

Giordano Bruno, *De Gl'Heroici Furori*.

WRITING / READING 1.   VIA BRUNO

"To cleave the general ear"
De l'Inghilterra, o vaghe Ninfe et belle
whom do we address o Nolano
reading in writing
at the opening of your beached furors
a heroic excuse
those darn white-blooded nymphs
my rigor cannot reach
through love sonnets where the arsenic bite
belabours the style

    thoughts / words
darkening (as I can) these pages
Cause, principle & unity
shown up shot values
& Giordano speaketh the vulgar tongue
puts his cards down
                  on this table
              book & notebook
             two eyes
to look with & through.
the image moves either way
unprivileged
"consider all this instead as being said indeterminately
(considered so even by those who by their authority can say it)
put down with difficulty
placed in the arena
the theatre
waiting to be examined

when the music has been arranged"

the line breaks
not writing
reading

something dubious, suspect & indendent
(shld read: impendent)

Jove, not taken as too legitimate
for once he was something else
& will be other again

composition dissolved
complexion changed
figure modified
being altered
fortune varied

every pleasure a definite transit

on the table book & notebook
journey & motion

Ash Wednesday   row on the Thames   walk thru London

"When they see a foreigner they become so many wolves & bears, by the Lord; they put on the malevolent look of a pig when you take away its trough."

two fantastic fooleries, two dreams, two shadows
& two quartan agues

criticizing the historical meaning

but what held me most was this, by one NW: "You cannot forget that which Nolanus... truly noted by chance in our schools that by help of translations all sciences had their offspring."

eyes red at dawn
the furors abated by no aubade
"ho forse in odio il sole?"
& therefore declared there to be many
& space to be infinite

it's the white around the image
reveals the image / caught staring

into the whites of my eyes
a space thus described, opens

WRITING / READING 2. VIA MICHEL FOUCAULT

"... the problem is no longer one of tradition, of tracing a line, but one of division, of limits; it is no longer one of lasting foundations, but one of transformations that serve as new foundations, the rebuilding of foundations..."

repetition of a theme
to avoid anxiety)
(& how to avoid
repetition to become
tradition
the necessity of
keeping it in mind
at hand at the moment
of composition,
   always
to be in sight of
the limits, their
periplos

                    we write
against & with   .
                         the music
I mean
the movement arises
from the twin wave

 : the body   (against & with)   history:

from their interaction, thought
from thought, action

"What must I be, I who think and who am my thought, in order to be what I do not think, in order for my thought to be what I am not?"

an/other
drunken boat
Rimbaud's espontaneo
advancing
- where else is there to go? -
so that poetry
may enter that region
where man's Other
becomes the Same as himself.

the given:
a body & a language

make their own plurals
& yet he talks of

an apparently inert density
a woof of darkness

gloom because   *"man is cut off from the origin that would make him contemporaneous with his own experience"*

not a cut in time
but the opening
from which all time flows
, & all things.

thus doomed to a strange stationary anxiety
the duty of repeating repetition?

"The only thing we know at the moment, in all certainty, is that in Western culture the being of man and the being of language have never, at any time, been able to coexist and to articulate themselves one upon the other. Their incompatibility has been one of the fundamental features of our thought."

where I disappears
in the vertical slash
a space opens

a space in which
I can think again
(sink again, sing again)

think again
a space of multiple dissensions
its purpose to map

change & transformation
a task is set
to think again

& contest the origin
of things; to create
an origin without beginning

to avoid repetition
to become
the necessity of time.

WRITING / READING 3.   VIA JACQUES DERRIDA

The names of Thoth

Theuth   hierogrammarian
        god of the secondary language
usurper   say the priests of Ra
                  you become creator
by metonymic substitution
     by historical displacement
          by violent subversion —

the way the moon replaces the sun, by pun
          the kiss (ionh)
               of the moon (ioh)
                    by permission of
his majesty the sun the essential
disappearance in place of which
Thoth the moon &
               writing.

The king's double, & the word's,
nearly identical, different only
from the sun as the sun's mask is
though who can look long enough
to tell the difference?

the essential attributes
the supplement
the representative
the stand-in
the repetition

"Master of the books"
secretary to the sun
hypomnetograph

Osiris' brother
'master of the divine words"

Sheshat his companion is
"She-who-writes"

"Mistress of the libraries"

first goddess who knew how to engrave
she marks the names of the kings on a tree
in the temple of Heliopolis
while Thoth counts the years
on a notched stick.

The god of writing is
(it goes without saying)
the god of death
who substitutes
the breathless signs
for the living word
& "numbered the days
of the gods & of men"

"The bull among the stars"

the figure of Thoth stands against origin
the father the sun the word
by supplementing it . By the same token
it takes shape, gets its shape from everything
it resists & replaces.
Turning upon itself against itself
the figure turns into its contrary, the messenger-god
a god of the passage, of the absolute passage
between opposites

I am my father my son & myself

he's the joker

    an available signifier
    a neutral card
    a "wild" card

    adding play to the play.

WRITING / READING 4. VIA CANGUILHEM

& Condillac's
claim that

dans l'odeur de la rose
la statue est odeur de rose

a fable has held
us in suspense
centred
here the living
is light & heat
carbon & oxygen
calcium & weight

here we miss
the story of
the female tick

an itch
's raison d'être
is in the
scratching

& poor Pascal knew
the Kosmos had blown up
his *eternal silence of the infinite spaces*
an itch he couldn't scratch

the tick too waited
for eighteen years
hanging on to the end
of a twig
waiting
for the smell of
rancid butter

& Pascal knew not
how to choose
between centripetal needs
& the demands of a colder knowledge
the tick hung on
Pascal was no longer at the centre
of the world

yet remains a centre
   (centre between two infinities
   centre between nothing & all
   centre between two extremes

& the centre is the state
nature places us in
the tick's accuracy not his
drifting on a vast middle
proportionate to only parts of the world
related to all he knows:

   "he needs a place to contain him
   time to last him
   movement to live him
   elements to compose him

        heart & food to nourish him
        air to breathe..."

spidered in a vast web of alliance
centre of this vast web of alliance

the tick falls

o infinitely paradoxical sphere of knowledge
centred everywhere
we are marooned in the margins
the great chain of being
a legiron links us to the centre of centre
in this crystal ball the snowflakes fall
when we rattle the chains
greek antecedents haul us in by

shade of Posidonius in Strabo & Ptolemy
geography the projection of Heaven onto earth
two-way system of correspondances:
geometry w/ cosmography yields the topographical
physics w/ astrology the hierarchical

rancid butter not enough
in the absence of a mammal's warm blood
the tick clambers back up
waits another eighteen years

universal sympathy, Pascal, is universal determinism
a vitalist intuition
influence
an astrological thought

& Buffon
via Paracelsus
speaks of the "tincture"
of heaven it takes

a man a long time
to receive

"La vie, disait Bichat, est l'ensemble des fonctions qui résistent à la mort"

while the natural philospher
his empiricism masking its theological foundations
the origin of positivist & mechanistic conceptions
of the environment
               is supported
by the mystic intuition of a sphere
of energy
whose action
at centre
is identically present & active
at all points.

& Newton read
Jacob Boehme & Henry More
found sustenance in the image
of an action's ubiquity
streaming from a centre.

WRITING / READING 5.   VIA ROBERT KELLY

"All past time is dream, and like a dream has no centre"

when the light comes on she finds herself
alone. the question is still the same:
how to be all one in the light.
the centre of my centre of nowhere.
there are voices, they talk, we answer

or talk back; no melody without
a suggestion . suggestion of lyrics, words
overdetermined noise.
      the music
goes on. plays. plays itself &
is played. I am played out on
the green felt meadow of the world.
the world fell. rests. One-eye stares
up from the felt place. One-eye
has always felt like blindness to me.
look at me. roll forth, marble
of the world, marvellous navel.
the single is mute, hides nothing.
strings of words. linked & not linked.
sounding the walls of the cup.
      When
the speaker comes on
I turn the radio off. Immediately
the light changes. the light changes
in the presence of the pen's nib.
      Other
links. I sniff the ink & find
memory to be chemical. invisible
molecules spell time backwards. but
memories exist only in the present.
the past is only the past when re-
membered in the present. this
saturday afternoon. day of chronos.
keeping time. keeper of. the feat
we have hungered after for so long.

WRITING / READING 6. VIA ROBERT DUNCAN

(his *"Empedoklean Reveries"* & Allen Fisher's letter on same)

the sphere
           could have been
                      water.

A body is nearly all water.
& a fire penetrated the sphere,
                separated it.

            What did it separate?
              What is a separated sphere?

& what, what was that fire?

           & why did the sphere
              if it was water
    separate
            instead of changing, of being
transformed
            as I witness every morning
                into steam?

Who could not abolish the sphere
            The kitten transforms
        the yarn-sphere
            the kitten is not fire
              could be fire
            to the yarn
    the lioness in the desert
        is fire
            to the zebra

      the lioness in the desert
          is water
              to the sun

the lioness
in heat
roars

I come
unstuck
in fire-water

        There is more than one fire
        It is the fire of love

           separates
      me from myself

          It is the fire of hate
      makes me whole

          against the other

Burning with love / burning with hatred
      I am transformed

          in anger I say
          you have burned me
          & I I
          was devoted
          to you

1.

Light a cigarette
in the heat of the battle

a burned offering
(to myself)
cools me down.

On my way

to the bookshelves
I change the music
then I find a text
on the text.

        A multiplicity of first elemts
his roots he calls them

            a rhizome of four
       the roots of all

            fire . earth . water . air

       equally alive, equally divine
       able to move & mingle
       to move in relationship to each other
       to mingle with one another

       (like) the basic colours on a palette
       with which the painter
       paints the diversity
       of all things

  : in the same manner one explains all
the phenomena that appear & disappear
without needing to call upon absolute
creations or absolute destructions
                one will
simply evoke & describe minglings &
exchanges between the roots.

Those are the elements, the elementals.

To move them
in relation,
two opposed actions
called
   philotes (love)   & *neikos* (strife)

but its is a complex machine
the elements themselves have sympathies
that will move them contrary to the love/strife dynamic.
& strife, or hate, by separating the dissemblances
does ease the meeting of the sympathies.
We

2.

Abandon the commentaries! Listen -
listen to the music

inadvertently

put on, what came
to hand as I walked to the shelves

it's playing now
as I read further
into Duncan's text
& meet the same
composer!

  What does it mean
  beyond coincidence?

Monteverdi's *Lamento D'Ariane*

      What labyrinth does the kitten invent
in its play?
          Can I or you follow it &
find the king, the
              "name of continuance"?

           The sphere has come undone.
      For love . She wants
  to find   the centre .

3.

I thread my way back
towards you
who work in the back room
to touch for a minute, to kiss you
Zahia, Gaia
before coming back
to this labyrinth.

           Walter Benjamin tells of
             the rhythmic *Seligkeit*
               the sheer pleasure
         Ariadne, or the cat, finds
          in the simple play/act
      of unrolling that ball of yarn.

The sphere of love   &   the sphere of hate
        who can lift them

the lioness
carries her cub
in the maw
killed the zebra

the human rears up,   vertical
               sinister
et dexter,
              two hands   one
either side of centre

lift up the spheres

burns both hands   of who is equally
          devoted to love & hate.

But I no longer see it clearly.
    But it never was that clear.

The sandals
forgotten
by mount Etna
tell us
nothing.

        The lion is no excuse for the human.

June 18, 1862 . Marx to Engels:
      "It is strange to see how Darwin, among his animals and his plants, recognizes his English society with its divisions of labour, its competitiveness, the opening of new markets, Malthus' 'struggle for life'… In Darwin the animal kingdom functioned like the bourgeois society."

Does this actually mean
that nature does not exist
or is but the fantasmatic representation
of the real social nature?

"All that is natural must have been born historically"

Ariadne is not my kitten

In the circus
I laughed with
the children
at the clown
who dropped
the coloured balls
I watched open
mouthed the acrobat
who did not
drop the balls
I admired
the lion who
jumped through
the burning
circle.

Fear? Yes, there was fear, too.
    It is always there.

        It will not let up . let me . stop
here.

      laugh at the acrobat
      fear the clown
      watch the lion

        eat the lion-tamer
            whose zebra-striped gala battle
          dress will be resown
        into a clown costume

          let me . stop .
here . the sun is out . that
sphere .

BODY COUNT

1.
as if visibility
skin-deep blackened
my blood
        he calls
as it darkens
for rain &
punctured skin
where flesh kneads
flesh, where
word-deep the salt-
pulse licks its
bounds,
        where deeper yet
she rains past the ciphered
corpuscules,
        parts their warsong.

2.
with two fistfuls of light
- two palms
        crossed with darkness -
we wove ourselves, did
we, or did we move
into the labyrinth
leaving the talked
to shreds outside
outside
        where it once belonged
wrapped in the muezzin's

call's
serpent skin we work
to shed to angel
our lives against all magic
carpet rides
cried lot
by democratic
lot.

3.
   the date pit
in the dark-red cavern
of your mouth
saliva quickened
word-rain drawn
sprouts
luminescent roots
press
against the mouth
open & closed.

                    I will wait
until the trees
have grown glottis-high
then I will scale it
with my ape-feet
then I will
climb up the imitation
serpent into
the great letter-
being
      leads to

the sentenced
sentence.

4.
              evening, the
trance-count
trickles
  out, on
the angel
interface
    (no
longer to stand
under the tepid drip
of meaning)
                  drum-
taut & brown she
erases the stretch
marks of
day.

5. "Dunkel ist das Leben, ist der Tod"
Great rusty barbs of being, each
& every terror an angel, an angry
stone thrown at the door, a child's
fist, wanting the speed of light—
getting the song of the sadness of earth
the genitive removals, those distances
between & those that clamp us in,
& the sparkling wine darkling in the glass.

THE BROKEN GLASS

1.

last night
you found
a wine
glass wierd-
ly broken not
a chip & not a
crack a near
perfect
break a
round of glass
½" thick
as if cut,
no way
could we have
thrown the glass
away
it stands
on my desk
the rim-ring
rests
vertically
on the glass a
circular band
a 90° angle
against the glass
a mere circumference
dipped
into its past volume
one
edge smooth-
ly sanded down
jagged

break-line
what
does it
where does it
if it does
it does!
mean I
mean connect
with our lives
this broken glass
strangely un-
broken
this glass
merely took
its rim away
freed its
mouth
from ours.

2.

after the glass you
found broken by
itself somehow
I broke
a pot, vessel of
earth, clay pot reddish
outside un-
glazed finish fired
in slow coal ember heat
does not - did not
I have
to remember it'
s broken now) hold
water, held
when it slipped

a ring
of yours -
but was more
than that
was the round
berber pot whose
circular rim
had four corners
climbed up
tight chalice shapes
meant to hold candles -
did not hold water
held fire in
stead light
a light of four
candles up
to our
nights.　　　One
candle arm
broke.　　　Clay
mixed with rougher earth
pebbles some
glass shards entombed
at centre raw core
　　　　　the fire

up-ended it
stands
on my desk
next to yesterday's
broken glass.
　　　　　I don't know
what it, again, does it
mean.

            Means.
for what . to what
end no longer
in sight.
                 march events.
                all ways
           find the way
              (find my way
pick it carefully
out from under
the shards
         to the text
to the heart of
the text-
ure of my life the road
is littered
with broken objects.

It's turning
into obsession this
transparent solid I'm
trying to make yield
             to force to birth
          sense into my
writing hand.

3.

The shape
retained
beyond
accident.

The rim-less
glass
still holds
water,

        knife
sharp edge un-
polished
rim re-

verses function:
put my lips
to the empty
glass

fill it
with me
blood of
my mouth

lips
cut
to over-
flowing

it will fill
with words
methedrine
nights

        bled
into this
vessel this cup I
have tried

not to call
can no longer
not call
a grail

a rimless cup
pure crystal thus
totally transparent
invisible.

To find it
you have to
fill it not
with water

not with trans-
parent wine,
put your
lips to it

then when full
of you
you finally
see it.

The grail is when
you see yourself
in the glass.
You

don't see
the glass.
The cut doesn't
hurt much.

The knights could not
find it. They thought
it would show itself
in great pain.

The pain is before
or after. The grail
is frail. Glass is
inbetween.

4.

           the clear ring
of purpose

is more
than I can pretend to
that clarity always
eluded me
have had to hold on
to various objects
have focussed my obsessions
- to go with them
that much faith
I have at times
mustered -
           that the obsession
leads me on
will eventually lead me
out, that there is more
than meets the eye.
A broken glass
meets the eye.
A wound happens,
to be healed
to be whole again
to stave off decomposition
to contain
the hole inside.

Shall I send it can
I send this ring
down there?
This glass can it
become lens
let me see
what is going on.

The rim settles
around the hole
contains it
keeps it
for awhile.

from: *make it up like say*

MEANING A MONKEY

you did what you didn't
it makes sense
years later he saw
how slow I am
he should no he
or are we all
but didn't
you did it makes
sense different
from moment
it always but does
mind's habit
meaning a monkey
back of mind
of course that's why
there are no other
I mean I knew then
had I known but
who could have can
tell me could it have
he had an
for everything
spilled milk
rents in the fabric
experience of vouchsafes
nothing we didn't

you well who was to
 hindsight blocked
 jeers
 nobody could have
 it's not my
 or yours it's just
 that meaning is
 just that after
 birth of experience
 and that
 just it like who
 could we certainly
 want to get
 on you can't look
 who is to see
 what is there
 you can't sue
 the real is
 what you make it
 up to be or not

*

make it up like say

    beauty does not exist
    it insists

    night owl shriek
    the ear answers

    a darker brown
    ink flux

    redraws the first letter
    it is not serial

could have been
pears   the hydrant

is another letter, that
city

You cannot add
owl shriek to

book stave.
"Image

is an act
not a thing"

mistake(n) synthesis
I know thee

not. in a darkened room.
Decisions

involve movement
not monuments.

imperceptible flight
Owl fright.

To cease the lure
to ease

it
adumbrate.

In the distance
irreducible

a language makes
it

Owl of beauty shrieks

five hundred books later
the car breaks down

so you aim for that effect.
so.

One circus closes down,
clown.

Total allergy syndrome.
Synecdoche.

1949, may, Paris:
Jean-Paul Sartre meets Charlie Parker

a scalloped or curved
outline

an indented deed
tooth act.

*

but the idea behind it
    remained just there.
    doesn't it always or nearly.
    we are nearly there and this
    is becoming a habit.
    the regular paragraphing of one's life.
    auto-identation clicks
    a dead sabre-tooth tiger dream

into tame place.
so time he says is an old saw
all teeth on one side
so what's new on the other.
and hot.
how many notches in yours.
time to call time
a simple bend in organ space.
how could that be she
basked on the tensile saw.
all mouth and no teeth.
a complex machine
that hollow round space
near spherical
chinks of time incrusted
in its base.
he speaks through it
and that is what
it takes,
plus a tongue.

*

but the a
abuts the other, o
how we move again
come here, winter
there, blue sun
peels a nerveless sky
a day like strawberry
jam on your cheek
crystals of cold marble
the other side of the glass
light, light
shovelled into bags:
did I meet you too in Saxony?

To open it up to Owlmirror,
a straight story, glass
and mirror
it is done
with, jerkily des
cending a stair
case,
        books & books
and inbetween
the kettle boils time
rhythms the juicer
does away with
the blood of the sleeping sealions
splatters the glass
becomes another mirror

PUT YOUR FACE ON

wake up along edge of
irate hunger a lack unease
& pull of light
remorse remodels thirst
the dream so clear it's useless
lost here found there fondled
know not where, known
a week ago held
your face indication of
useless hold over and into
palmolive sunday presents
from the body shop these
birthday bones to be picked
over breakfast snap out
of skin your mind
revs engine of not worth
depression craters moods

lift out of ! I say rise
a new ice age lily
once only Greece and Turkey
now here no common flower
now here no common name
only the millennial
patience to be found
comes clear you will
too hunger for death
no hunger at all
a desert flower roots in 1950
propagation by bulbs
only sometimes flowers
rare beauty the beauty
bountiful
switch off the light
do not search for mirrors
Castiglione broke all hers
that is not you
what is is you
movement through
a changing landscape
like a life a lie
nothing stays the same
nothing therefore not interesting
catalyst is old destruction
it lay there til picked up
something added brings change
a shove in the direction of
direction like old chaos
is gas then gas is
other is controlled
for a time and then it is
undone like man
it's a gas & that
the solid past now

NEW POEMS

YEARS AGO, TUNISIA

from here on out they conquered
or that's what movement is called by some

second movement. Sonata in B flat
history of Kairouan in the blue vault.

a star and you play dice
but night conquered that colour long ago

two towers left brique arabesques
to the left a voice and a human tape

the star doubles over the pain of
fire in fig water carries over the years

Ludwig you are she said sad in this piece
further on quantity and speed of in the dice

the captured table makes it easy velvet disposition
deposition (the) carries over from here to where

this machine
is a father's skull-egg
bending the blue
of a sky
that is not yours
& sets in motion
a handwriting
tries to recognise
itself
in the distance of
an afterlife
Nobody may ask
whose   The machine
never breaks down
the sky
holds its empty
promise no ink
takes on it
but takes it on
You need a hammer
to hear
what is not said
he keeps sending
the grey smoke
into the bone idol's
hollow
hells

THE TIME FACTOR IN SCIENCE FICTION MOVIES

That is as far as I'm willing to go.
You should always have one I on the page.

A greater time span is needed however
to put the first spring flowers into a vase and

yes one can learn to swim this late in life.
The war started this morning

in the afternoon I went swimming. Carew made light
of this wet blanket of a text

since death is common to all.
"Yes, but what's that

spiritual & immortal substance breathed etcetera"
The data can of course be the surprising

absence of perception. Someone who is
not here postulated an object

with something masking it. It also
goes correctly hollow when it is not a face.

CARTE DU TENDRE

before we were wrong
the maps were there

now they change all the time
if you are fortunate enough

to return to earth
come with me or don't

the skeleton returns, turns
enemy control interferes

the old biblical aims the names
hyperspace isn't a fiction yet

he wanted back to his world
their names and objects

pavements of a royal road
maps a pockmarked crust

a skin shot through both ways
no need to report to the monitor

the future is blue-ice
our major laboratory a direct hit

now calculate god's true size
there is a chamber inside

the eternal war
don't you understand

let it happen now
get into the car

if you want to get back
take the roads with you

the maps aren't any more accurate
though there are more of them

they feel compelled to write
a monster into each one

ORE BEFORE IT IS DRESSED

for Allen Fisher

a fabric fish basket perhaps
I bind & probably cross

activity exerts regular intervals
strength to do at the crossings

perform a system of lines
the transference of interface

cross produced by a motion
he binds an interrelated sanskrit

the point of application of
froth or foam caused by fermentation

dice designed for cheating
everything possessed or available

a system of electrical conductors
between more than one path

free of all charges &
designed to entrap

protect confine carry divide
the sweetest cloak you can conceive

opposed to gross possession
all gaps make it look like new

on assigned frequencies
clean pure bright control

a miner's work is difficult
excluding all tare & tret

his accustomed means of
a hand-made three-sided structure

development or completion
a gradual process of hammering

WINDOW PUN

red undulant
flat this that
magenta after
noon glass

austrian swallow
breathes abstract
strength
hoarfrost

enhance this
line's silence
strained shadow
on panes ankle

deep dew that
trained shadow
spectral drum
anhk on panes

does sever
this lie
space cracked
clouds

bring snow
ream of silence
dream to some
further part of

this place of
real space
real that is
not here

not today no
snow made it
so yet made so
by this ob

stinate us
electric light
grows rehearsal
the prompter

sharper etches
a more solid
mood the loose
stage state of

this script that
quadrupelfuge the
comparative mode
will lose grip

day's over
before out
though there be
keeping on

despite all
no other way
to tall time
tell-time

some the end
has forgotten
sandal slipped on
slid off

sun struck
flint on horizon
acute time girth
for the going

the end forgotten
has some disre
membered mode
hide light in dark

hide beginning
the second movement
before the first
that soul caught like

this old look
forward further
from herewith
where no thing

guillotined a lace
curtain nothing
yet to be seen
Guillaume

Apollinaire turns
off Seely Road
hides the light
among lights

as ever passes
Amen Corner
hurries towards
the end of

the coda lizard's
Broadway a safe
brown paper bag
"this is you"

he said pointing
out the window
a tale fooled
by a pinch

of salt we shall
cut the talk
begin the heart
of the thing

tucked under
his arm
the scales fell
where all go

if when from
his eyes the
window faithless
wills it so

the trees scream
murder
those comets
the end remains

severed there here
ere long
darkness fell
a short distance

away "Queen of Spades"
kept and kept at
bay by the
fierce cone

of this light
that circle's
the perfect
rhyme the lines

stand revealed
where where
shivering burst
their thin veneer

that syntax
is what happens
when you heap
your will

against absence
thinner & thinner
the images lie
a palimpsest that

"leave it"
through the wall
voice bricked over
"lay it

aside" nobody
I would know
drain the red
the irrigated

voice no magenta
afternoon this
that flat glass
swallow

abstract breath
leave it
its enhanced
silence

in the sink
for tomorrow
to fill
it up again

ENGLISH LANDSCAPE

for Michael Palmer

In the King's Head the moves are from out to in. Five drops of rain on Echo Lake. The same occasions, whether offering themselves innocently enough or grasped at from too much experience, have never worked out. At one point there was this, well, Palestinian, you know, he drove a 6 litre Buick and the sky clears again. It is just a question of looking away. It is a question of timing your impatience. A sentence here a sentence there. So why should we find fault with content being paraphrasable — except that such moves leave a stranded whale. Last night's peremptory dismissive statement, metaphors for a certain England, an uncertain man. There is a test going on, it is a game in which the players are in white and the rain eats the light. Should I wait now or go on? It is a question of how you don't stop at the boundaries of a national language. Someone said I know what province he comes from but not what country. From Hellas to Barbarians, he said poshly. The middle or working class actually speak English, this fugitive cant. He's a foreigner Dr. Johnson. Make it up like now. Anyway, one perception impossible. Green-grey light, make of it voices. Careful the door remains. It does not matter that it is half open. What counts depends on where you sit. I stood up. Do I go searching around Woollies, pay much more? The dentist is called King, not Johnson. Drives a Jaguar and comes from Pakistan or Guyana. Patterns heard of. Open to imitation, not servile: a proffered path invites a walk. Of course a machete continues to terrorize English speech or else cuts this green light like chopped parsley.

TADPOLE STRATEGIST

sickness catches more than breath
this dim light catches further down
here the fertilized egg recapitulates the unthinkable
when the kappa comes out of the water it catches cold
when the waters break the kaulquappen roar
& the heart beats beyond endurance there
where our midnight shadow recapitulates noon
a crisis teaches us nothing though we know what it is Ed
a situation where we use force as a means of communication
a crisis teaches us nothing though the question remains
tadpole quantum jumps or
how does a communication become a command
direct translation exacerbates distortion
"to invoke in a willed shadow the unsaid object
with allusive words reducing themselves to an equal silence
contains an attempt at creation"
freedom arose from the eye of the storm
common origins shared with a world born of chaos
that was Saint Juste speaking)
& with man who weeps at birth
holy justice holy terror
a far cry from where I felt I was going
I went feeling a sense of foreign bodies
dissymmetry between offence & defence says Clausewitz
keeps wars from being total all the time
rest but not assured
the heartbeat had been irregular a sign of life
the kappa too thirsts for inclusion
our resistance spells that intrusion

DHÛ'L-RUMA

A willed emptiness, then breath.

Is it that the east wind has revealed
– the way writing, folded, spreads –
brown shards of a dwelling
clearing the sand hid its traces
sand the changing breath first duned
but now uncrests, disperses...

& the figure thus trimmed down
from an asymptote towards nothingness
arises expectation, the
held breath . Hamza , it sticks
in the throat, as sand does,
glottal stop, held
breath. That's
how high
the stakes
are.
   How high the dunes were.
He wedges all feeling
between the ephemeral & the invariant
that two-faced dog.
      In a permanence of shards
the master of ceremonies
passing through
envies the stalking
awâbid, wild
creatures of the desert:
those that last
even without memory.

GERMAN LANDSCAPE, REVISITED

well-hung
with yellow pears, a
mountain of wild roses
drags
the land into the lake
you staunch swans
you're loaded
with kisses
you drop
your heads into
the sacro-saint spill.

Goddam
it all where do I score
in winter
for flowers where
for sunshine
& the shade the earth
throws?

The walls they
just stand there
speechless & cold
the wind
in vain chases
the weather.

FIN-DE-SIÈCLE IDENTIKIT

for Thomas Meyer

This is my age
this is what Sibelius wrote at 36
sibilant Sibelius easy
lure easily
resisted twisted towards
another mood
this is no longer 1901
cannot transcribe it
this his second symphony
am pulled in by number
dirt dangling from roots
(no number is pure number –
the root of this century
dangling pull it up
never liked what his music
but listen to the craft
of exact number
raft of an age
godtack days when an
english sun belies
the upstairs bedroom
where you lie
empty & full of
the drug of sleep
the day passes
from one room to the next
pass the book discarded at
midnight drink wine pass
water pass the closed door
pass the salt the bread
some vomit with ease
some put it away
where it hurts

Sibelius's fin-de-siècle
syllabary,
Tom's gift, who made
bourride with aioli
two years running, stuck
as he is in Arcady,
a green place, not finnish
not english, "every holy Muslim
child's idea of Paradise"
you dream of it now upstairs
while here afternoon audience claps
incongruous world in concert
back now to Ives Webern Nono
the records mouldered
by English weather mushrooms
colonize the rifts
and valleys of his master's
voice as french a word
as this wine is italian
have no celtic
sense - lied that once -
teuton, not teton either
that boringly dutch
flat minds need
genever to curve the
horizon where
Vincent's ear rises & sets
apocryphal son
like words fingers in a
dyke he was
I am told
an anabaptist had
to flee
the Lowlands made Basel
this made-up ancestor
down through the
Middle Kingdom's water-ways

on hasty rafts of what wood
& heard & didn't hear
Kaspar's story
blind leader of a berber caravan
I speak in voices
always always
other people's voices
a thousand mouths
on this Gorgo-head
& now have let the I
out will
stand by it for a minute
will whisper into the sun's
ear my care
"to write
"every day
"to drink wine
"every day
"two actions
"hold me
"a vertical
"vertigo
"a matter of
"spines
"&
"esses
"smooth
"curvatures
as in this Mosel glass
a grape garland
lightly grasps
the rim
as I grasp at any
straw my luck
my vocabulary
deserts me
before it slurs

ALDEBARAN
ALDEBRAN
plucked that luck
or star from your shoulder
rode with it upcountry
on a raft made
from the skin
of our teeth
wrote it to its
source & the source of
the water was the same
as the source of
the skin it poured
from the pierced
lobe of the solitary
ear a flesh-jewel set
in the horizon's
curve a vista listens
to a voice the background
music still Sibelius
a fakeness there
a prettiness
our age no longer
holds distrusts as
much as the night
upstairs, upstars
darkened room at noon
as 300 years ago
the raft out of Amsterdam
beached in Basel
a fast film a life
of preaching a single-minded
community
the death of one Joris
so feared by the burghers
of Basel he's the only
3 years post-mortem

auto-dafé on record
the light of that pyre
sings in Vincent's ear
as we collide on
a curved now near
circular event
horizon now
the violins are
shrieking maggots
crawling towards
the end of another century & now
the 2 am news brings
tidings of
this fin-de-siècle
Menschendämmerung
outside.

THE HORSES OF LALLA FATIMA

1. MEDITATION IN A KITCHEN

      Out here where-
in the roads
fork
    we do too
the roads we
go down
        necessity's
passe-montagne
pulled tight
over the
eyes.   To see through & choose
weird boast
like poking one's eye out,
meaning in.
        (Con-
fusion of
movement : you can have it
if you want it
both ways . I eat
with a fork) I

risked the road
yesterday, will risk it
tomorrow . tonight
we rest in the oasis

of this kitchen
(a needed rest:
    "nothing ever is
acquired"
        proud boast
forgot about
biology, ir-
reversible
processes,
shorter breath
as the lines are,
get,
the lives.)
Heartcoals in a kanoun
movement at
& of rest, love
prepares a feast, lamb
roast in the oven, a tale
to be told, to be-
hold on
the air.

    the time
it takes the meat
to take : let's make use of
the time we have
    carefully, accurately,
(the hours you spend
    oiling   washing   drying
      your hair:
your patience, your
accurate sense of)
    your body against my impatience
      my rotting teeth
    no longer all that long
the length now of my lines
the enormous ambition

whittled down
to the voice of
the lyric,
box-canyon song
where the horses
rear, narrow ears
pricked, nostrils
flared towards
where the puma
prowls.

    Circling the meat
in the oven : the time
it takes -

(the way
those muscles we call
the mouse, *la souris,*
musculus & mus
- a cooked etymology
as in "to cook the
books" -
tighten under
heat, then crisp &
shrink back
down the
bone
    /
       white splinter-glimmer
grows a handle
on our lives
of bone & words & yes
we make what we make
as bony as our lives it
turns & stops & yes
control means loss.
It does   choice does

    & yet is the only choice
we have .
               Turn the roast
touch bare rocks
eternal snows &
in passing touch
& rest
at the crossroads
where we cross our
eyes to Hermes . touch to
go on from
the feel of the land
your thigh's
gentle slope.
There is strength left
in
the bones
& right there
in your
hands.
        It is all
I . we
        need it all.

2. THE TALE

          crosses the road,
last rays   long days   the
talk not of hope
more practical or
as they say
(who's they?
down to earth
(who'd dare
talk *down*
to earth?
(under the surface
not the earth's,
ours, or under our
talk's fastidiousness)
we are just that
& more
anchored here in smell
of roast in
your hand's accurate
mobility.
        Now
this story happens
when the prophet's
only daughter,
the mother of
Hassan & Hussein,
she who is called
Lalla Fatima
sent a caravan
of horses from
Mecca to Medina
(or maybe it was
from Medina to Mecca
we don't know
when it happened,
was it before or after

Muhamed's death, before
or after her sons
were born?) it does
not matter. This
matters : the horses
lost their way
(or the drivers
did, this again
the story does not tell
it was a human not
a horse committed it
to memory)
& when the sun had set
& their allotted time was up
& they had not returned
(how the parenthesis
flourish, how
the processual
stalks
from every direction
at once while
this art demands
again & again
choice at the cross
roads) which is
how I got this
story / I talked
of crossroads you
thought of the story
of the horses
of Lalla Fatima
as answer to my exegesis
on the fork (not
the one turned the roast,
the one in the road
where those eyes
were offered
to Hermes)

close parent
thesis, open to
where Fatima
in long flowing gandoura
anxious on rooftop
looks out over the battlements
of Mecca or Medina
(a tall house, her father
a rich merchant-prophet)
towards Medina or Mecca
where the straight road
has been forked
by the will of the horses
& Fatima now fetches
a fat-bellied pot with a
narrow opening she holds
over the kanoun where-
in burn the seven
consecrated perfumes:
black & white frankincense
elemi resin
wood of aloes
coriander
amber & myrrh.
Into the cleansed
vessel a handmaiden
pours spring water &
now both women
with the gathered tips
of their fingers raise
the pot & Lalla
recites a poem a
prayer & lo
the pot turns it does
a sure way you
say a sign points
out the direction
where-

in something
has been lost (let's
use you say
one of ours
that way, I wondered
what we had
lost, was coy, said
it is the earth
turns & our pot
may be from
the right place but
is not in
the right place
& who am I to
attempt practical
magick when I have
such a hard time
with the simple
telling of the story
which is my job
& then you
remembered more,
re-
membered the
mouthed words (which
you say are the story
you told me)
& I went with the fork
of the Greek road
where myth is
the mouthed words make
(or do they make)
the pot turn.
I wanted more, felt
something here I didn't
grasp, pushed you &
you called your
mother

who said there were
no horses
they were camels
but they did
get lost
& so the question
returns as:
where are the camels
of Lalla Fatima?
Or should I change
the title, re-
write the story?
No. This is
the story of
the horses of Lalla Fatima,
the horses that didn't
come back at day's end.
Or did as the pot
turned, or came
back as
camels.
The pot could not foresee
that fork in the
narrative road.
Down one prong
the horses rushed,
up the other came
the camels. Fatima
is surprised, she has
waited all these years,
the pot in hand
shatters, the prophecy
come true, the
horses are back as
camels. we are
none the
wiser.

POSTFACE

The first edition of this book, published by Francis Van Maele's Editions PHI, came out in Luxembourg, Toronto & New York in 1987 — the year I moved back to the US. For reasons beyond my control, the book was not widely distributed here in the US, except from a cardboard box in the back of my car — a time-honoured, honourable, but rather ineffective method of making a publication visible. So much so that when in 2001 Wesleyan University Press brought out *Poasis (Poems 1986-1999)*, they could boast that theirs was my first major book publication in this country. It is therefore a pleasure to have Skylight Press reissue *Breccia* both here in the US & in England where the book never had any distribution, though a good two thirds of the poems were written while living in London, and owe much to the company of the poet friends who were among the founders & players of what came to be known as the British Poetry Revival.

This new edition, besides correcting some typos & minor layout problems, has allowed me to adjust a few mishaps — two poems that were inadvertently dropped from the original books when these were inserted into the 1987 edition have been reinstated. Otherwise the book stands or falls as it did back then: my reasons for the gathering & the exclusions are laid out in the original preface, reprinted here. My friend & teacher Eric Mottram's introduction is also reproduced; rereading it I can only thank him again for his generosity of spirit — & register the pangs in my heart & mind & the gaping hole in the euro-american poetry community his untimely death have caused.

The cover painting — an antlered, Blakean figure — is by Allen Fisher, a work he offered me years ago & which has hung on the walls of my various dwellings these last 25 years. As Allen was the publisher of *Antlers*, selections from which open

Breccia, it is only fitting that his painterly meditation on the subject should become the cover. Thanks are due to him for gifts of the spirit & an enduring friendship.

Let me close by adding the front matter of the first edition: Grateful acknowledgement is made to the editors and publishers of the magazines and books in which most of the material in this volume has previously appeared. With the exception of a few previously unpublished poems, the poems in this volume have been selected from the following books: *Antlers I-XI* (New London Pride Editions, 1975), *Hearth-Work* (Hatch Press, 1977), *Tanith Flies* (Ta'wil Press, 1978), *Body Count* (Twisted Wrist, 1978), *The Broken Glass* (Pig Press, 1980), *Make It Up Like Say* (Fig Books, 1982) and *Net/Work* (Spanner, 1983).

Pierre Joris,
Bay Ridge, Brooklyn,
15 October 2014